DRAMATIC MEASURES

Bardolf & Company

DRAMATIC MEASURES
Lessons from a Life in the Theater

ISBN 978-1-938842-43-6

Published by Bardolf & Company
www.bardolfandcompany.com

Cover design by Shaw Creative
www.shawcreativegroup.com

For my mother, father, and Dad

and all the people in the theater and film industries
who taught me so much of what I know.

Other Publications:

How to Mess with Others for Their Own Good

All typos, redundancies
and grammatical errors have
have been put into this book
intentionably for your enjoyment
in finding them.

DRAMATIC MEASURES

Lessons from a
Life in the Theater

Chris Angermann

Bardolf & Company
Sarasota, Florida

CONTENTS

The Child is Father of the Man
  —William Wordsworth

PROLOGUE

CHILDHOOD MEMORIES

At some level, all art is personal. So, let me begin with five stories from my childhood.

When I was almost four, I saw my father play the Devil in a Christmas pageant. It was put on at the Waldorf school in Bremen, Germany, where he was a teacher. The play told several Biblical stories, including the creation of the world and the expulsion of Adam and Eve from Paradise. My father acted the role of Satan. He wore a black outfit with horns on his head and a big, long tail, which he waved around like a snake. Although he hissed and cavorted about the stage and scrunched up his face trying to look evil, I didn't find him terribly scary.

&

After my parents got divorced, my mother and I lived with her parents in Coburg, a small city in northern Bavaria with a picturesque castle on a hill. At some point, I attended the production of a children's play at the theater/opera house, a large, neoclassical, sandstone edifice with Baroque interior. I don't remember the name of the play, but in the second act the hero and his friends, a group of spunky teens, traveled to the moon. A large white screen descended

9

at the front of the proscenium stage, and miniature versions of the characters ascended into the rafters. I suppose it was done with puppets and strings, but at the time, it felt as real as magic, and I was enthralled.

&

For a season or two, my mother wanted to be an actress. She took lessons in a class taught by a retired professional actor that met in a small castle in the midst of a pine forest, two miles out of town. For a culminating project, the group put on a shadow play of *Hansel and Gretel* and my grandmother took me to see it. The actors performed behind a scrim which, lit from behind, showed their silhouettes on the white surface. I knew my mother was playing the role of the wicked witch, but when she appeared, I didn't recognize her. With her stooped figure, stringy hair, and warts on her beak of a nose, she looked like an evil hag. And she was really scary.

&

Before I entered grade school, I participated in a production of *Snow White* put on by the local amateur theater in conjunction with the sports club I belonged to. I played one of the seven dwarfs. There wasn't much space onstage and we were jam-packed behind the curtain. When it parted, we had to slide down to the floor and arrange ourselves at the feet of the princess for the opening tableaux. I didn't have any lines, but I was proud to wear a red dwarf hat and a long beard as white and fluffy as cotton candy.

&

When I was five, my mother gave me a puppet theater for Christmas. The hand puppets had hollow heads made of soft, molded plastic with a hole in the bottom where I could stick my pointing finger to make them nod. Thumb and middle finger went into the arms of the simple dresses draped from their necks, allowing the puppets to gesture and hold onto things. The ensemble included a king, a princess, a policeman, a witch and, for some reason, an alligator. I made up fairy tale stories and performed them, playing all the parts and using different voices. My family and friends were appreciative audiences. Needless to say, many of the mini-plays ended with the alligator devouring the other characters.

I got to be actor, director, playwright, and impresario. Who wouldn't get hooked on that?

All the world's a stage,
And all the men and women merely players;
They have their exits and their entrances,
And one man in his time plays many parts.

—Shakespeare, *As You Like It*

INTRODUCTION

I spent nearly 20 years as a professional theater and opera director in New York City and at regional theaters in the Eastern United States. When I decided to change careers and become a writer, editor and book producer, many of the theatrical skills and lessons I'd acquired carried over into my new line of work.

Having worked with set and costume designers turned out to be excellent practice for guiding book cover and layout artists. Dealing successfully with a wide variety of plays made it easy to tackle new projects—I can work in different genres with ease. Whether I am producing a children's book, a how-to book, a memoir, a volume of poetry, or a mystery, suspense, romantic or historical novel, I figure out what's required to create a high-quality, professional product and proceed accordingly.

Learning to fashion a visual narrative onstage allowed me to put together photography books which tell a story in pictures from page spread to page spread. Helping playwrights develop dramatic storylines proved invaluable for guiding fledgling novelists in the plotting of their tales. Creating rounded characters is a similar process for plays and prose fiction. An ear for dialogue, honed in the theater, has proven useful as well.

Because of my thespian experiences, I am comfortable spending long hours to make sure everything works while remaining open to last-minute changes to improve the production. I make it a habit to return phone calls promptly. In the theater, if you wait too long, the job that might be yours will go to someone else. I know to show up even when I don't feel like it. As an actor, if you're really sick, it's okay to go to bed and cure yourself. But if you're well enough to be up and about, you're well enough to go onstage. That's what's expected. The show must go on.

All arts encourage curiosity. As an interpretive artist, you never know when you might be able to "use" something you've done, felt or observed. During the time I earned money as a temp in New York between theater gigs, I always told people, "I'm doing corporate anthropology," and they'd laugh. But studying how lawyers, accountants, bank executives, secretaries, office managers, and other working professionals behaved under pressure was all grist for the mill. I have put many of those observations to good use both onstage and on the written page.

Above all, theater attuned me to different audiences—what they're looking for, what turns them on and off, and what they need to know to "get" what you're trying to tell them.

When I directed Ibsen's *A Doll's House* at Playmaker's Rep at the University of North Carolina in Chapel Hill, I had an instructive experience on opening night. In the third act, Torvald Helmer (played by David Whalen), desperate that his wife was leaving him for good, challenged her, "Have you no religion?" When Nora (Jenna Cole) replied plaintively, "I do not exactly know what religion is," there were gasps in the audience.

I was amazed. Having lived in New York City and New Haven, Connecticut, both liberal communities when it comes to politics and religion, I had no idea that the lines would shock anyone. It was my first experience of the Bible Belt and gave me insight into its values and just how radical and upsetting Ibsen's play must have been for the audience at its premiere in Copenhagen in 1879.

When writers want to hire me now, I always ask, "Who is the audience for your book?" Nine times out of ten, they'll say, "Everybody!" Which often leads to a fruitful discussion about niche markets, how few people still get their information from physical books, and the fact that over 70% of American readers are women. This is especially important for non-fiction writers. You'd think they would figure out ahead of time who might be interested in their ideas, but only a few take the time to do so.

For me, the theater was an excellent training ground and provided a smooth transition to my career as a wordsmith and producer of books. But I have noticed that others—both amateurs and professionals who succumbed to the theater bug for a season or two—have benefited as well. The actors I met in New York, temping like me, seemed to have more on the ball then many of the regular employees. If they worked for a company longer than a week, they would often receive offers for full-time positions.

Of course, there are obvious cases of stars and entertainers profiting from their time spent onstage or acting on the silver screen—Ronald Reagan comes to mind; as do Arnold Schwarzenegger, and Al Franken (before he resigned his U.S. Senate seat); and yes, as of this writing, Donald Trump, who treats the White House and the presidency like a reality TV show. They all made use of what they learned as performers. Reagan's presence and ability to appear natural in front of a television camera, to speak as if he were communicating directly with his audience, did not come without considerable practice.

But many others, not as famous or high-profile, have parleyed their theater experiences into other professions with excellent results as well.

I did a play at the Amateur Comedy Club in New York City, a private drama venue that hired professional directors for its play and musical productions. The club included attorneys, bankers, business owners and corporate executives. Located in an old carriage house in the Murray Hill section of Manhattan, the intimate theater was on the first floor. Upstairs had a small kitchen, a lounge/green room, and lockers where members stashed their booze.

The play was Alan Ayckbourn's *Absurd Person Singular*, a farce dissecting middle-class angst by showing the foibles of three couples as they socialize at each other's suburban homes. One of the husbands was played by a 30-something vice president of Chemical Bank, then the third largest bank in the United States (it later merged with Chase and took its name). He was a busy guy, married with two young children, and his wife "allowed" him to participate in one production a year. He had started acting for fun but soon noticed that it had a positive impact at work as well. Because of his thespian pursuits, he was able to conduct business meetings with greater confidence and vocal command.

A similar thing happened to my son, Erik. When he was 11, he was asked to present a local politician with an arts award at a banquet where a number of important people were in attendance. By then, he had participated for several years in an after-school program run by Florida Studio Theatre (FST) in Sarasota, where I worked as Associate Director of New Play Development.

Erik displayed a confidence in front of the crowd that surprised and pleased both my wife and me. He received lots of compliments and took it all in stride. A year later, he told us that he didn't want to do the theater program anymore. He wanted to play ice hockey! We were happy to support him in that endeavor, too, although his stage exploits did not prepare him for dekes and body checks on the ice. Today he is an engineer, and I remain convinced that his easy-going confidence in public goes back to his time spent in FST's youth acting program.

Why does the theater offer lessons for so many of us? Perhaps because acting is deeply embedded in our human experience from the time we were young children. Who hasn't played "doctor" as a kid, or put on mommy's hats, scarves and heels, and stalked across the floor like a little giraffe? It's how we fantasize, dream and learn about aspects of the world we haven't encountered yet. Being able to walk in others' shoes is a good thing, and the stage gives us plenty of opportunities to do that and more.

&

This book, then, contains my adventures in the theater and the life lessons I drew from them. I trust they will prove helpful to actors and directors starting out in the profession—I certainly wish someone had explained them to me beforehand.

I also think they can be useful to people in other careers. If life imitates art, perhaps the process of creating art can offer valuable lessons in a variety of non-theatrical situations—at work, at home, with friends, children and life partners. Theater and film are labor-intensive, relationship-heavy fields—just look at the credits at the end of movies these days and you get the idea of how much collaborative work is involved. Anyone engaged in activities that unfold over time, which require an understanding of process and an ability to deal with a variety of people and personalities, can benefit from these lessons.

Here is a simple example with complex ramifications: When I started to work at FST, the artistic director, Richard Hopkins, told me that I wouldn't fully comprehend the job until I had spent two seasons there. The first would give me the lay of the land of a busy, hectic place. The second would clarify what happened as a matter of course and what was due to accidents, luck and unexpected occurrences. He was right, and I imagine the same holds true in many other jobs.

I understand that some of the material may be too detailed for people not familiar with the specifics of the theater and film world. To make things as clear as possible, I have provided thumbnail synopses of the plays which were significant in my journey and development. And I have followed the suggestion of a successful, public speaker: *Never make a point without telling a story, and never tell a story without making a point.*

Well, not exactly. I admit I haven't always observed the second half of his advice. Sometimes, a good story is its own reward.

Of course, no book can replace the real thing. Learning by doing is an essential aspect of any performance art. That's what rehearsals are all about. The English word "rehearse" at its root refers to dragging a harrow repeatedly over the ground, digging deeply into the soil. In German, the word is "proben," meaning to practice or try out. But we don't have to reinvent all the spokes in the wheel by trial and error every new generation. Some things can be passed on verbally. I couldn't be a writer if I didn't believe that.

So, for students and practitioners of the theatrical arts who wish to expand their repertoire and practice—

for theater and movie buffs who like to learn more about what goes into the making of a show and what goes on behind the scenes—

and, for those rare individuals who want to expand their horizons beyond where their interests have taken them so far.

May you all be edified and entertained.

Chris Angermann
Sarasota, Florida, 2019

DRAMATIC MEASURES

*I never let schooling
interfere with my education.*

—Mark Twain

ACT I– TRAINING

THEATER SCHOOLS

Many undergraduate theater programs in the United States are staffed by former actors, dancers, directors and tech people who have traded the uncertainty of the life of an itinerant artist for the comfort, safety and regular salary of a tenured college professor.

Male actors often leave the thespian hustle early on. Raising a family is hard when you're living hand to mouth trying to "make it." In the old days, artists had patrons. When I was in college, I met a playwright in New York, whose wife was a psychiatrist. She brought home the bacon and supported his theater habit while he acted as a house husband and pursued his artistic career—an early example of a post-feminist marriage.

But even in our more liberated times, men feel the pressure to be the providers for their families. That's why young leading men are a dime a dozen, but good middle-aged and older actors, as rare as a buffalo nickel.

I was a third-year student at the Yale School of Drama (YSD) when I auditioned my first professional cast in New York for a production at the Yale Repertory's *Winterfest of New American Plays*. The piece was *Coyote Ugly* by Lynn Siefert, also a student at the drama school. We were both novices, so it was a good thing that Lloyd Richards, the Yale Repertory Theatre's artistic director, was at our side, helping to guide us through the casting process. A well-known adage in the theater is that 90% of a successful production comes from casting the right actors. Lloyd was there to make sure we started off with that advantage.

Set in the Arizona desert, *Coyote Ugly* is a dark comedy about a family with incestuous tendencies. When Dowd, the prodigal son, comes home for a visit, his 12-year-old sister, Scarlet, lusts after him and does her best to get rid of his new, city-bred wife. Lynn's characters and language are quirky and require the ability to play larger than life. We had several good choices for the younger characters, but we still needed a 50-something actor to play the father and were getting worried. The handful of candidates we'd seen were woefully inadequate.

Then Ed Seamon walked in. He looked weathered and worn, yet had a sparkle in his eyes that hinted at barely contained mania. It seemed as if he'd come off the pages of Lynn's manuscript. At some point during his audition, which confirmed our initial impression, Lloyd turned to me and whispered, "Thank you, Ed Seamon, for staying in the theater."

Lloyd knew from first-hand experience how many talented actors leave the professions after pounding the pavement of New York for a season or two without success. We were glad that Ed had stayed the course.

Some who tire of the grind go into theater education and end up teaching undergraduates. This is a good thing. One of the first to do so was an influential British director, Ben Iden Payne, who had worked at the Abbey Theater in Ireland, Stratford on Avon in England, and on Broadway where he launched John Barrymore's career. He also mounted productions at a number of American Universities and spent the latter part of his life at the University of Texas at Austin. His memoir, *Life in a Wooden O*, is well worth reading.

Like the regional theater movement, which started in the 1950s and spread professional theater beyond New York City to the rest of the country, the proliferation of undergraduate majors has benefited American film and stage. Unfortunately, in the early days, only a few of the instructors were of Payne's caliber. The rest were mediocre, rested on their modest laurels, taught outmoded approaches, and didn't bother to keep up with the latest developments in cinema and the theater. At best, they encouraged talented young actors to pursue a career in the arts, but they rarely inspired or taught much material that was relevant.

Fortunately, that has changed, as many undergraduate theater departments now hire educators who continue to keep a foot in the professional world as actors, directors and playwrights.

Graduate training programs were a different world all along, certainly at elite institutions like The Juilliard School, NYU's Tisch School of the Arts, Carnegie Mellon School of Drama, and YSD. Most of the teachers at these schools were practicing professionals. In the case of Yale, New Haven's proximity to New York ensured that many of the professors and instructors regularly worked on and off Broadway, in large regional theaters throughout the United States, and even in other countries.

Add to that the high caliber of students, picked from the cream of the candidates—YSD has more than 1,200 applicants each year for the 60 or so available slots—and you had a fertile, artistic environment all around.

At least in theory.

MY TIME AT DRAMA SCHOOL

I attended the Yale School of Drama at a time when the institution and I were both in transition. I had spent five years as an English teacher at High School in the Community, a public, alternative school in New Haven, where the faculty members made up their own curriculum. Having written theater and film reviews on the side for the *New Haven Advocate*, a bi-weekly community newspaper, I was familiar with what had been going on at the drama school and the Yale Repertory Theatre.

At the time, Robert Brustein was Dean of YSD, but he preferred to spend his time and energy as the artistic director of the Yale Rep. A venturesome producer, he put the theater on the map by inviting talented actors and directors who created bold, audacious productions. He mounted well-known classics in non-traditional interpretations, offered musical plays by Bertolt Brecht and Kurt Weill, like *The Rise and Fall of the City of Mahagonny* and *Happy End*, and introduced a slew of brand-new works. He scheduled American and world premieres of plays by Edward Bond, Terence McNally, Christopher Durang, Arthur Kopit and Sam Shepard, which challenged and, in many cases, offended the more traditional New Haven audiences. If you haven't heard of these playwrights, don't despair. Most of the spectators hadn't either and didn't like their works; and there was the rub (as Hamlet would say).

Having a true repertory theater, in which several plays run in rotation, required a company of actors to commit for an entire season.

Those who returned as regulars year after year did double duty as acting teachers at the drama school.

I saw many of those Rep productions as an undergraduate at Yale and, later on, as a theater reviewer. They were off-beat, demanding, zany and inspired. I remember *The Frogs*, a musical adaptation by Stephen Sondheim of an ancient Greek comedy by Aristophanes. Performed in the Yale Gym's swimming pool as an aquatic romp, it made quite a critical splash (pun intended). The cast included Meryl Streep and Sigourney Weaver who were students at YSD at the time.

Alvin Epstein's production of Albert Camus' *Caligula* had a young Christopher Walken as the insane Roman emperor scuttle like a tarantula up and down on marble temple stairs that extended across the entire stage. The production was a revelatory walk on the wild side and a harrowing descent into madness and death. Andrei Belgrader staged Shakespeare's *As You Like It* as if the Marx Brothers met Alice in Wonderland on their way to the forest of Arden. Needless to say, the Bard's language took a backseat to the antics, but the production did capture the frolicking, madcap Elizabethan spirit brilliantly.

There were misses, and all-too-often a director's concept overwhelmed the play. *Man Is Man* staged in a boxing ring revealed nothing about Brecht's claim that you can turn a milksop into a blood-thirsty, wartime killing machine. *The Sea Gull* performed on a silvery floor that mimicked an ice rink did little to illuminate Chekhov's play. It might have been interesting if the actors had made their entrances and exits on skates, but they didn't. What it all meant remained a mystery. Brustein directed and cast his wife Norma as Madame Arkadina, the older actress who has seen better days, and she was not up to the role.

As an aside, it's always tricky when male directors cast their wives. Their personal relationship often blinds them to certain qualities of their spouses, and the performances suffer accordingly. But that's another story.

After a decade of such adventurous theatrical fare, the Yale Rep had an international reputation, but the local audiences had fled in droves. More seriously, Brustein had neglected the drama school, inflicting mediocre teachers on the acting students. The design department, led by Ming Cho Lee (sets), Jane Greenwood (costumes) and Bill Warfel (lights), was outstanding. But the acting program was considered a joke. At the time, the word in the entertainment industry on Yale actors was: They can't walk, can't talk, but you can always count on them to do something interesting. When Brustein came up for tenure, Yale University, priding itself as an educational institution, did not renew his contract.

I arrived at the drama school in 1980, a year after Lloyd Richards took over as dean. During the transition, many members of the third-year class felt abandoned and dressed up like 1950s beatniks, adopting the attitude of a lost generation. Some of the stories they told about the previous regime were damning. One student described to me a first-year acting exercise in which the class spent the hour fording an imaginary river and picking golden apples from the trees on the other side. Not exactly a way to hone your craft.

An experienced director, Lloyd had first made his name with the Broadway production of Lorraine Hansberry's *A Raisin in the Sun* and was known as an excellent play doctor, too. He had been running the O'Neill Theater Center for some years, developing new American playwrights. August Wilson, a Pulitzer Prize winner for *Fences* and *The Piano Lesson*, often acknowledged Lloyd's pivotal role in his success. Lloyd was also a superb acting teacher.

Taking up the reins at Yale as dean and artistic director, he faced two big challenges: 1. How to bring back audiences to the Yale Rep and 2. How to return the drama school to its past glory.

He addressed the former by eliminating the repertory approach and offered well-known plays in straight runs, mounting works by Shaw, Chekhov, Ibsen, O'Neill and Shakespeare in productions that focused on the plays rather than the directors' concepts. To nurture new playwrights, he created *Winterfest*, a mid-season, mini-repertory festival of new American plays.

He also developed a productive relationship with Athol Fugard, the South African playwright, actor and director, and scheduled a number of his plays, including the world premieres of *A Lesson from Aloes*, *Master Harold and the Boys* and *The Road to Mecca*. Although conventional in structure and presentation, Athol's plays were politically and morally charged, exploring the ravages of Apartheid on ordinary people, both black and white. Never strident and often poetic, their deep humanity resonated powerfully with audiences.

And the subscribers, pleased with productions they could appreciate and enjoy, returned.

It was my first lesson in how important it is to pay attention to one's audience in terms of social, economic and political demographics. In New Haven and at Yale, that meant a liberal, educated, academic, language- and text-oriented, upper-middle-class crowd. If you ventured too far afield, exploring unfamiliar, avant-garde territory, they were unhappy, lost interest and voted with their feet by not showing up.

To improve the drama school, Lloyd hired Earle Gister as associate dean. Earle had an outstanding record as an administrator of theater education institutions. Under his leadership, the programs at Carnegie Mellon and NYU had both thrived. At Yale, he kept the faculty members that had something genuine to teach and gradually replaced the fossils and dodos with new blood. When the first-year acting class lost confidence in their instructor, he stepped in and taught scene work using plays by Ibsen and Chekhov to lay a foundation in naturalistic theater. Earle focused on one thing and one thing only—What does the character want?—and insisted that students make moment-to-moment, active choices. By the end of the year, everyone in the class played action as a matter of course.

For the playwriting program, Earle hired Oscar Brownstein, whose philosophy was: You can't teach playwriting, but if you expose good writers to the play development process with actors and directors, they can learn. Personally, I think that's wishful thinking. Few prose writers make good playwrights. It's far better to take people who actually have talent in that most rigorous of dramatic forms— playwriting—and nurture them.

Oscar did have one rule I still applaud. To nip clichéd efforts in the bud, he made certain locations off-limits. Students could set their plays anywhere except in kitchens, living rooms, bedrooms, dens with TVs, pubs and bars, or on park benches. Having to come up with new venues forced them to be inventive.

I personally benefited a great deal from Oscar testing out his theories. In a collaboration workshop, all first-year directing, playwright, acting and dramaturgy students were divided into teams and tasked with turning a short story into a play. A few experienced playwrights—David Hwang and David Ives—did very well. For the rest of us, it was like the blind leading the deaf. Fortunately, the faculty weighed in when we got in trouble and helped shape the works for the final workshop performance.

Being older than most of my classmates—I was 30 when I arrived at YSD—I made sure to soak up everything the school had to offer. As directors, we participated in many of the acting classes— voice, movement, fencing and scene work. During our first year, we had to assist a third-year director's thesis project; in our second, a professional director's production at the Yale Rep. I signed up for double duty both years.

I took Wesley Fata's movement classes for two years, instead of the required one. With my intense schedule, I knew it was essential to stay in good physical shape. Wesley had a Martha Graham based approach which, like Pilates, strengthened an actor's body and core but did not show up onstage in mannered performances. He had been the assistant choreographer on the original Broadway production of *Hair* and, in the class before the Christmas break, delighted everyone by teaching the "Be-In" dance from the musical. At some point, he complimented me on making more progress than any other directing student he'd ever had. Although I was pleased, I knew he set the bar for directors quite low.

I spent my Christmas vacation at the first *Winterfest* working as assistant stage manager to Frank Torok on Sybille Pearson's *Sally and Marsha*. The two-character play chronicles the unlikely friendship between two women who are apartment neighbors in Manhattan. The director, Robert Allan Ackerman, had made his name on Broadway a year earlier with Martin Sherman's *Bent*, a drama about the Nazi persecution of gay men starring a young Richard Gere.

It was instructive to watch the play development process conducted at a professional level. Ackerman was superb at cutting unnecessary material and rearranging sections of scenes with the two actors, Robin Bartlett and Frances Conroy. But he treated the playwright like a fifth wheel, banishing her to a small desk far from the directing table and generally ignored her. Frank dealt with this situation by becoming the "daddy" of the production. He told jokes and performed silly little jigs to lighten the mood in the rehearsal hall when things got testy. He took Sybille out for drinks after rehearsals since Robert usually rode the train back to NYC right away. In large part, because Frank kept things on an even keel, the actors stayed relaxed and the play was a success, moving to New York where it ran for 56 performances at the Manhattan Theater Club.

Each year I was at the drama school, the faculty improved. Debbie Hecht became the voice teacher and actually knew what she was doing. Leon Katz, a debonair man close to 70 who sported dramatic eyebrows, came to lecture on theater history. His classes were filled with stories, wit and an encyclopedic mastery of the subject. I found his approach to play analysis from a dramatic point of view brilliant and inspiring. Leon used his wide-ranging knowledge to encourage us whenever he could. I remember one of my fellow directing student asking him if, in the absence of a large cast, using puppets to create a crowd scene onstage could work. Leon arched his salt and pepper brows, pretended to think for a moment and opined, "Well, the German director, Erwin Piscator, staged the Battle of Borodino that way in his 1963 New York production of Tolstoy's *War and Peace*. I think you'll be fine."

My second-year acting and directing teacher, David Hammond, brought on by Earle Gister, was a gifted dramatic verse instructor He had taught at Juilliard and the American Conservatory Theater (A.C.T.) in San Francisco, where he also directed. David quickly realized that the actors in my class did not have a grounding in basic techniques. So, he gave us all a crash course in sense memory, affective memory, and animal exercises before tackling Shakespeare and, later on, Shaw, O'Neill and other playwrights whose heightened use of language presents unique challenges.

It turned out that I came to the drama school at the perfect time for what I needed. I had applied in part because I wanted a safe place to learn how to work with actors—safe in the sense that I could fall on my face and not have to worry about it hurting my career before it ever got off the ground. I met with plenty of opportunity there to bloody my nose.

Although the school was in transition, there were many talented students who have had successful careers since. I worked with

Frances McDormand, best actress Oscar winner for *Fargo* and *Three Billboards Outside Ebbing, Missouri*, John Turturro, Angela Bassett, Roc Dutton, Kate Burton, Sabrina Le Beauf, Cordelia Gonzales, Laila Robbins, Reg E. Cathey, and Jane Kaczmarek. Dereck McLane and Catherine Zuber, who designed the set and costumes for my thesis project, have both since won Tony Awards. Rick Butler, who created sets for me at the drama school and early on in my professional career in New York, has been production designer on such TV shows as *Person of Interest* and *The Enemy Within*.

In workshop productions of plays by David Ives, Bennett Cohen, Lynn Siefert and Keith Reddin, I first cut my teeth on new play development and learned about dramatic and narrative structure. Dramaturgs Rick Davis and Michael Zelenak provided further support, helping me edit and prepare texts for rehearsals and productions.

During my three years at YSD, I directed two cabaret shows during the school years and acted as co-artistic director with Rob Barron for a season of the Yale Summer Cabaret. In the latter, we required everyone in the company to go onstage at least once. Many of the tech and administrative staff were game and enjoyed playing the robbers in my adaptation of Shakespeare's *The Two Gentlemen of Verona*. Our talented lighting designer, Steven Strawbridge, was less sanguine but made a memorable, one-line, walk-on appearance as a cop in my production of Jean Cocteau's *Orfeé*, a surrealist version of the Orpheus myth, modernized even further by Lynn Siefert.

When it was my turn to go onstage, I did a one-night stint as the corpse in Tom Stoppard's *The Real Inspector Hound* and played Kid Gleason, the hapless manager of the Chicago White Sox, in the world premiere of Rusty Magee's *1919: A Baseball Opera*. The piece dealt with the Black Sox Scandal, in which eight of the Chicago team's players were accused of throwing the World Series against the

Cincinnati Reds in return for money from a gambling syndicate. Having been to a number of AA baseball games of the West Haven Waves, an Oakland A's farm club, I had witnessed many a manager dressing down an umpire and used my first-hand knowledge to develop my character. I even got to sing a solo in a musical number!

During the school year, I worked on new plays by fellow students and did two workshop productions of my own choosing, including *Lear Dream*, an adaptation of *King Lear* that focused on the heath sections where the monarch goes mad before reconciling with his daughter Cordelia. When Roc Dutton in the title role gave himself to Shakespeare's language, it affected him physically, triggering unexpected gestures and actions, and I understood for the first time how well the words of a great dramatist will carry you and lead you to surprising discoveries.

At the suggestion of David Hammond, I chose *The Bewitched*, by English playwright Peter Barnes for my thesis production. A satirical farce about the doomed reign of Carlos II of Spain, the play is a mad cauldron of gobsmacking spectacle, rip-snorting comedy, mock Elizabethan language, British vaudeville turns and musical numbers adapted from songs from Hollywood movies (more about all that later).

I decided to be the first director in my class out of the chute and mounted the production in early fall. That freed me up to do another new play workshop of a musical by David Ives about Harry Houdini, the famous escape artist, and to direct my first professional production at *Winterfest*. In the spring, on my second professional outing, I was able to put what I had learned to good use, helping first-time playwright John Heller to structure his one-act, *No Trains for Harris*, and directing it at the Philadelphia Festival for New Plays.

Attending YSD was one of the great experiences of my life. I had oodles of fun and learned more than I ever dreamed I would.

In addition to a basic grounding in acting and directing, I came away with a number of invaluable lessons on how to develop as an artist and work with other creative people.

I was pleased to attend graduation—I had skipped my college ceremony in an act of youthful protest and defiance. A contingent of my classmates put on Groucho glasses when the Drama School students were officially recognized. A press photographer snapped a picture, which made it on the front page of the *New York Times* the next day.

It was a fitting conclusion, appropriately silly and dramatic, to a splendid three years, and I felt ready to tackle whatever might come my way in pursuing a directing career.

&

My advice about going to graduate drama school is:

- Look for inspirational teachers.
- Seek instructors who practice what they teach and stay engaged with their art.
- Let them teach you craft and learn by observing them in action.
- Be a sponge.
- Take big chances and don't be afraid to fall flat on your face.
- Trust that your talent will emerge if you nurture it and give it room to breathe.

INTERLUDE

What Is a Dramaturg?

Most people without a background in the theater have no idea what a dramaturg is or does. No, it's not fantasy action figure carrying a pouch of power tokens in an Xbox video game; although a good one will come armed with a bagful of useful and esoteric knowledge about all aspects of the theater.

When I started out at the Yale School of Drama in 1980, dramaturgs were even less well known. LMDA, the Literary Managers and Dramaturgs of the Americas, wasn't founded until 1985.

Some of my fellow directing students shared that general ignorance when they first encountered dramaturgs in the play adaptation project during our fall semester and had little use for them. One called them "dilettantes on parade," good only for getting coffee. He was both unkind and off the mark, and his dismissive mindset said more about him than the people he mocked.

It turns out that what dramaturgs do goes all the way back to the ancient Greeks. In the *Poetics*, the earliest surviving work of dramatic theory, Aristotle distinguished between comedy and tragedy and analyzed all the elements of the latter, including character, plot, action, and speech. He also gave us concepts like *mimesis* (imitation or representation), *catharsis* (purgation of emotions that evoke terror and pity), and *hamartia* (the fatal character flaw of a hero that

34

leads to his downfall—the excessive pride of Oedipus, Achilles' belief in his invincibility despite the vulnerable heel he gave his name to, and the uncontrolled rage of Hercules, the Incredible Hulk of his time.)

Dramaturgs taking an active role in theater and opera productions originated in 18th-century Germany with Gotthold Ephraim Lessing, a playwright, philosopher and seminal literary figure. Since then, dramaturgs have become versed in theater history, dramatic theory and the nuts and bolts of how traditional plays, musical scripts and opera librettos work. They also can be very instrumental in new play development.

On one of my trips to Germany before the wall came down, I visited East Berlin and did a pilgrimage to the Theater on the Schiffbauer Dam, home of the Berliner Ensemble, the famous troupe founded by Bertolt Brecht after World War II. There was no one at the front office, so I sneaked into the main theater and was surprised to see the company in rehearsal. I took a seat in the back row and watched.

The cast was going over the scene from *The Mother*, a play Brecht adapted from the novel by Maxim Gorky, in which the title character agrees to support a general workers' strike. At some point, someone noticed me, and the dramaturg came over to ask me what I was doing there. I explained that I was a theater student from the United States and would love to stay and watch for a while. After a brief discussion with the director, he said, "Okay." (They must have figured I was harmless and not some government spy sent to make sure they weren't doing anything subversive.)

Following a run-through of the scene, the actors gathered onstage, and I expected the director to give notes. He didn't. Instead the company embarked on a lively discussion, led by the dramaturg, about the history of unions and how wildcat strikes were dangerous, leading to participants getting beat up by the police, and in some cases, killed; and that in parts of Africa and South America there were no unions at all to protect workers. The actors asked questions and contributed their own knowledge. This went on for about 20 minutes. (Germans are nothing if not thorough.)

Then they ran the scene again. I didn't see much difference, although one of the actors seemed a bit more cowed at the prospects of going on strike. I marveled what you can get away with in government supported theater—rehearse for months on end and talk about everything under the sun.

But it was clear that the dramaturg played a significant part in the proceedings, more so than in any American theater at the time.

Over the past 30 years, that has changed in both theater and opera. The role of dramaturg has grown, often overlapping with the job of literary manager. Depending on the venue, dramaturgs may write program notes that provide historical and cultural context for productions, hire actors, help pick a season, assist directors in rehearsals, edit plays and librettos, help develop new plays and playwrights, and more.

Some directors can act as their own dramaturgs. My second year at YSD, when I assisted Lloyd Richards on a production of *Uncle Vanya*, he told me a story about directing Lorraine Hansberry's *A Raisin in the Sun* on Broadway. Apparently, there was one scene that didn't work and Lorraine kept rewriting it without success. Finally, with opening imminent, Lloyd and his stage manager spent a night taking lines from all the drafts she had written and rearranging them until they added up to a viable scene. The next day, they presented their version to her, not sure how she would react. Lorraine, who could be formidable, was surprised and not at all pleased, but she read their pastiche. Then she said, "We will use this scene. But don't you ever do this to me again!"

When it comes to play preparation, it is always useful to have another set of eyes or a different perspective. In my experience, first-rate dramaturgs provide that. Their advice can be invaluable, and I had the good fortune to work with some of the best from the get-go.

I met Rick Davis my first year at the drama school when we teamed up with a playwright to adapt a John Steinbeck short story. Rick was smart, hard-working and had a great sense of humor. Later, he helped me prepare the text for my workshop production of *Lear Dream*, the heath section of *King Lear*, and trim the script for my thesis project, *The Bewitched*. The latter is a play of epic proportions, with over 40 characters, and we had to do some serious pruning to make it work with a limited budget and cast of 18.

Fortunately, Barnes was a Baroque writer, who loved to embellish and never could resist a good joke. We managed to cut several scenes and pare speeches without damaging the narrative coherence, and we eliminated several characters altogether. In one scene, we reduced the number of Spanish grandees on the royal council from three to one and gave their lines to the players that remained. Leon Katz had assured us that doing so would strengthen the surviving roles, and he was right—an excellent lesson that continues to pay dividends in my current editing work. We spent the summer preparing the script for the fall production. It was a fun collaboration and worked well.

Rick told me early on that he wanted to be a director, and that was the career he pursued after drama school with great success. He has staged numerous plays and operas, served as artistic director of the Theater of the First Amendment, and taught at George Mason University where he is now the Dean of the College of the Visual and Performing Arts.

A more critical situation when dramaturgs saved me from disaster occurred during my first professional outing while I was still a student, directing Lynn Siefert's *Coyote Ugly* at the Yale Rep's *Winterfest*. I had staged the play in a workshop production at the drama school with Frances McDormand as Scarlet and John Turturro as her father. That summer, it received further development at the O'Neill National Playwrights Conference. When it was selected as one of the four *Winterfest* offerings, I told Lloyd Richards that I wanted to direct it, and he agreed.

The play was still unfinished—one purpose of *Winterfest* was to give playwrights the opportunity to complete their works. Lynn did several rewrites and hit a wall. She had the end, a wonderful visual moment when Scarlet, after getting rid of her brother's wife in the desert, has Dowd put his ear on her head to listen to her thoughts. But Lynn didn't know how to get there and resolve all of the characters' stories along the way. None of her versions worked, and I was unable to help. My own writing and editing abilities were still in their infancy.

As we got closer to opening and the pressure mounted, we were at an impasse and behaved like a bickering couple whose relationship is on the skids, with separation and divorce looming on the horizon. Fortunately, Lloyd stepped in. He had seen this happen with another student collaboration at the previous *Winterfest* and knew what to do. We met in his office along with the two faculty dramaturgs, Joel Schechter and Michael Cadden. Lloyd assured Lynn that they would help her finish the play and told me to focus on working with the actors and staging. Lynn and I both felt relieved and agreed to go on.

I was unsure how to deal with the tension that lingered between us and asked David Hunter, an old New Haven friend and mentor, what I could do. He suggested I get Lynn a small present with a nice card and write that I continue to believe in her and her play, and that together we would knock it out of the park. Which is what I did.

Lynn read the card, threw her arms around me, and gave me a big hug. From that point on, we worked together as a team again.

I learned a huge lesson about how scared, desperate people—myself included—cover up their fear with anger and aggression when they're really crying for help. They just don't know how to ask nicely. There is a broader message here. The hardest moments in a marriage or working partnership occur when both parties are at sea or down in the dumps, and demand support from one another. They often turn into Macbeth and Lady Macbeth after the murder of Duncan—two people desperately clawing for help, yet completely unavailable to each other.

If you're ever in such a situation, you're not going to find the solution on your own. You have to go outside the relationship for help.

As far as the production went, we got away with it. Lynn continued to work on the play afterward, and *Coyote Ugly* had its world premiere with the Steppenwolf Company in Chicago. She later wrote the screenplay for one of my favorite Disney movies, *Cool Runnings*, the story of Jamaica's first bobsled team at the 1988 Winter Olympics in Calgary, Canada.

Getting back to dramaturgs: the good ones are knowledgeable, caring and informative about a myriad aspects of theater and playmaking. If you have the opportunity to work with them, consider yourself lucky and be sure to show your appreciation.

And you never know, they might even bring you a cup of coffee.

The Rin Tin Tin method (of acting) is
good enough for me. That dog never worried
about motivation or concepts and all that junk.

—Robert Mitchum

ACT II–ACTING

WORDS AS ACTION

In Shakespeare's plays, characters say what they mean and mean what they say. Even Iago, that great dissembler and manipulator who presents a likable exterior to hide his evil intentions, tells us in asides and soliloquies what he is really up to. When he flatters Othello or deceives Desdemona, he uses words to suit his purpose. He may have vile motives, but even when he lies outright, he takes a straight-forward approach rather than an emotionally shaded one.

Characters in Shakespeare use words as actions to directly affect others. Words are their tools, their instruments, to persuade, convince, seduce, dominate, etc. How well they wield them is part of the pleasure of the dramatic experience.

That is not the case with Ibsen, Chekhov and most modern playwrights. Characters often say one thing and mean something entirely different. Mundane conversations are laden with heavy emotional baggage. People try to get what they want from one another using words, but the language itself doesn't necessarily match their purpose. In the theater, what is really going on underneath is known as subtext. Actors still play actions, usually expressed in active verbs—to flatter, persuade, hurt, empathize, elicit sympathy—but the words don't necessarily say so.

This development entered western drama after the Romantics discovered the interior self, a minefield of confusing feelings and emotions. Since Sigmund Freud investigated the mechanisms and workings of dreams and showed how the unconscious operates via transposed images, visual and verbal puns, and slips of language, we know that people reveal their motivations even when they are not aware of them.

When I taught English at High School in the Community (HSC), a public alternative school in New Haven, the superintendent, Gerald Tirozzi, came to talk to the staff. We were a teacher-run school and had successfully resisted his attempts to install a principal by calling on the parents of our students to battle on our behalf. Usually, a handful of dedicated, determined protesters on the steps of city hall or at the education department did the trick. That day, Tirozzi meant to extend an olive branch. He complimented us for doing an excellent job—we knew we did—and said, "For too long HSC has been treated by the rest of the school system like an abortion." We all looked at each other. He had meant to say "stepchild" and quickly corrected himself, but by then he had lost any credibility with us. As far as we were concerned, his Freudian slip had revealed his true feelings.

As an actor, you have to understand the implication of words and how to use them to impact others. Proper training will boost your ability to do so.

Vicky Hearne, an American philosopher, poet, essayist and animal trainer, wrote a fascinating book, *Adam's Task: Calling Animals by Name*. One of the chapters, "How to Say Fetch," is a discussion of authority and intention. If you give the command and don't mean it, an alpha dog will know it and refuse to obey you. You must act like Patrick Steward as Captain Jean-Luc Picard on *Star Trek: The Next Generation*, who says "Engage!" as if he means the word to propel the Starship Enterprise forward on its own. Every young actor and director should read Hearne's chapter.

Interestingly, words as action in dialogue are making a comeback because of Marvel and DC comic book movies and TV shows, and the popularity of Sci-Fi as a genre. Take any episode of *The Orville*, Seth MacFarlane's recent homage to the Star Trek sagas, and you'll hear such lines as "Our deflector shields are down to 27% and failing," or "Impact in 15 seconds!" Nothing is going on here except the passing of information, albeit hysterically; although good actors will say even these lines with the intention of affecting the other characters in the scene.

Mediocre actors will just shout the words and make them sound like the filler they are. A computer-generated voice would have the same effect. I'm convinced the relentless underscoring in movies and TV shows—tense, throbbing soundtracks for suspense, schmaltzy synthesized violin and cello music for romantic scenes, etc.—has become all-pervasive to drive home the meaning and generate an emotional response that no longer comes from good writing and acting.

Saying lines like you mean them is easier when scriptwriters use words that reverberate. Plosives—sounds formed by consonants that stop the airflow, such as P, K, T, G, B and D—give added oomph to an utterance. "Pusillanimous pussyfooters" and "nattering nabobs of negativity," phrases coined by speech writers for Spiro Agnew, Nixon's belligerent, pit-bull vice president—the Donald Trump of his era (though not as effective)—have a greater impact when spoken out loud than when read on the page. Say them with gusto and you will feel an immediate jolt of energy.

Great orators know that words can have a powerful emotional impact and use every rhetorical device and aural trick to heighten their delivery. Good actors do, too.

Words can rouse and rile feelings. Many people understand that but don't want to take responsibility for doing so. It's why social media and the Twittersphere have become so popular. They allow people to be outrageous, flagrant, provocative and mean-spirited without having to own their words.

It is a cowardly practice and doesn't change the fact that they're miserable human beings. Their angry outburst may give them a temporary high, but they don't improve anyone's life, least of all their own.

ACTIONS SPEAK LOUDER THAN WORDS

There is a simple, fun theater exercise in which one actor gets the word "Yes" and the other, the word "No." Armed with these monosyllables, they take turns trying to convince each other to say the opposite word. Anything goes, with the proviso that actions causing physical harm are off limits.

It is a great way to teach subtext because it requires active engagement. Actors must hold on to their own purpose against repeated assaults by their opponents while pursuing their own objective. You can see subtext in action as the two participants cajole, tempt, entice, hector, plead and harangue one another. Sometimes the exercise ends with them shouting at each other in frustration because they're not getting anywhere.

Only rarely do the antagonists manage to succeed using just words. The two most ingenious winning strategies I'm familiar with were both physical. In one, the actor saying "Yes" took out his wallet and put down a $10 bill, asking "Yes?" With each "No" response from his scene partner, he upped the ante, adding another Hamilton and repeating, "Yes?" When he got to $50, he stopped, pointed to the small pile and offered once more, "Yes?" Then he reached for the bills as if to pick them up, and his opponent buckled. For a penniless drama student that was more than chump change, and he acquiesced. It was a cunning, if not exactly cheap way to win.

The other was a young man who had to get his female partner to say "No." He hit on the strategy of slowly unbuttoning her blouse. The devious part was that when he asked "No," she had to keep saying "Yes," encouraging him to go further with each turn. When he started to work on her bra, she had enough and slapped him with a resounding "No." He was pleased to have won, although she packed quite a wallop.

The lesson: Actions often speak louder than words.

In fact, many people operate that way—a good Samaritan guiding someone out of harm's way, a friend putting a hand on an agitated pal's arm to calm him, parents beating their children (not an endorsement), protesters provoking violent confrontations.

The phrase, "Sticks and stones may break my bones, but words will never hurt me," attests both to the limited power of words—otherwise, why bother making the comparison?—and the greater harm that violence and bodily force can inflict.

There are historical traditions acknowledging that most people won't remember words nearly as well as physical actions—not what they're told, but what is done to them. In medieval times when the guild system prevailed in Europe for artisans—carpenters, masons, butchers, bakers, candlestick makers—the day an apprentice became a master craftsman, his teacher-mentor would give him a hard box on the ear so he would remember the special occasion for the rest of his life.

We have graduated to less violent rewards to provide lasting reminders—medals, diplomas and other forms of tangible recognition—and that's a good thing.

But the notion that we should look at what people do rather than say continues to be important. Words matter, but often, both onstage and off, actions speak louder than words.

BETWEEN THE LINES

In Shakespeare's *Henry IV, Part 1*, one of the scenes takes place in the Hogs-Head Tavern where Prince Hal and Falstaff and his merry men are carousing. With civil war brewing in England, the king has summed Hal, his wayward son, to meet with him the following morning, and the young prince is understandably nervous. To reassure him, Falstaff suggests that they play-act the scene. He will take the role of the king. Installing himself on the throne, a chair placed on a table, he proceeds to scold his son.

As the "royal" audience proceeds, Hal gets frustrated by Falstaff's bombast and says, "Dost thou speak like a king? Do thou stand for me, and I'll play my father."

Falstaff agrees and they trade places. In the process, he challenges, "Depose me? If thou dost do it half so gravely, so majestically, in word and matter, hang me up by the heels for a rabbit-sucker of a poacher's hare."

When the prince seats himself on the throne, he says, "Well, here I am set."

On the page, this exchange takes just a few lines. But in the theater, it becomes a complicated sequence of stage business. The fat, drunken knight wobbles precariously on the table and needs help from his gang members to make it safely to the ground. In contrast, Hal leaps nimbly onto the table and takes his "rightful" place on the throne.

It's a multifaceted visual sequence. Young Henry shows himself ready to be king, ready to supplant his father upon his death. At the same time, he displaces his mentor and friend, foreshadowing the heartbreaking scene in *Part II* when Falstaff approaches him, and Hal, now King Henry V, cruelly rejects him:

I know thee not, old man. Fall to thy prayers.
How ill white hairs become a fool and jester.

This is not a case of actions speaking louder than words, but of action informing words with additional meaning.

It is also why treating Shakespeare as a theater poet in English Literature classes misses out on a great deal of meaning that comes to light in a stage production. Shakespeare, after all, was a great dramatist who understood plays as theatrical events, not just as a series of beautiful lines.

Such multi-layered, foreshadowing moments occur in our lives and dreams, too, although we usually don't recognize their implications until much later.

A female friend once let on that, at her wedding when she walked down the aisle to the altar, she tripped by herself and almost fell. Instantly, the thought flashed through her mind, "If it doesn't work out, I can always get a divorce." Which is what happened when she and her husband grew incompatible. At the time, she chalked up the moment of doubt to her anxiety as a bride, but in retrospect, she felt that her body was trying to tell her something she was unable to admit to herself—that things wouldn't go well. It was only a brief stumble, but a prescient one nonetheless.

There are other examples of things happening between the lines—quick looks passing between lovers or long gazes shared by married couples that communicate worlds of mutual understanding.

Ever since Marlon Brando's instinctual performances in *A Streetcar Named Desire* and *On the Waterfront*, it has become the norm for actors to do a great deal of their acting between the lines. We have come to accept this performance style as true to life.

For comparison, take a look at the 1932 film *Red Dust* with Clark Gable, Mary Astor and Jean Harlow, the original platinum blonde. Then watch *Mogambo*, the 1950s remake, also with Gable, but this time with Ava Gardner and Grace Kelly as his female co-stars. You'll see the difference, both in script and execution—more talk in the earlier version, and more pauses in the latter.

Rent any 1930s screwball comedy—*The Front Page*, *My Man Godfrey* or one of the *Thin Man* movies with William Powell and Myrna Loy. The performers talk a mile a minute and leave hardly any pauses between their lines. The verbal banter commences at a breakneck pace. Interestingly, more recent TV shows, starting with Aaron Sorkin's *The West Wing* and continuing with the comedic banter in Amy Sherman-Palladino's *Gilmore Girls* have returned to this practice, creating rapid-fire exchanges between characters that eliminate all pauses between lines.

In contrast, check out Robert Duvall's performance in *Tender Mercies*, or Robert De Niro in *Taxi Driver* or *The Godfather, Part II*. De Niro has perfected the art of minimalist film acting, yet a lot goes on behind his laconic exterior and between the lines. The fact that he can also go broad in comedies and mock himself—in *Analyze This* and *Meet the Parents*—shows his range and how deliberate he reins in his performances in serious dramatic roles.

Both current and past approaches work well when executed by talented actors. Although they represent different methodologies, reflecting different attitudes about what is considered "realistic" or "real," great acting will transcend any particular style.

PINCH-OUCH

There are lots of approaches to acting—Lee Strasberg's Actor's Studio and The Method, Stella Adler, Michael Chekhov, Sandford Meisner, Viola Spolin, Uta Hagen, to name a few.

My favorite is the "Pinch-Ouch" Theory.

If you pinch a child, chances are you'll get an immediate "ouch." If you pinch an adult, you might get a different reaction. Unless you really squeeze hard, most grown-ups will ignore you or delay their response until they've thought about what message you are sending and how they want to deal with it.

Acting requires being like a child, taking in what you get from another actor and reacting spontaneously without interposing your mind or thoughts—Pinch-Ouch. A performance results from stringing all the pinch-ouch instants together moment-to-moment. Another phrase describing this approach is "Acting is reacting."

Of course, there is more to the craft than that. Soliloquies, people talking alone onstage to the universe, the furniture or an invisible rabbit, are another matter. Many actors in sci-fi and action movies have to perform opposite monsters, aliens or Transformers, which aren't there during shooting. Sometimes there are tennis balls, flags or other stand-ins to help them figure out where to look. Their adversaries get inserted later on with computer-generated imagery (CGI).

In a July 9, 2019, *New York Times* interview commemorating the twentieth anniversary of the movie *American Pie*, Eugene Levy recalled shooting the scene where he surprises his son, played by Jason Biggs, having sex with an apple pie. "For me it was more anti-climactic than one might think," Levy said. "I walked into the kitchen and I was only looking at a piece of tape marked on a light stand where my son would have been humping the pie. So, I had to react to a piece of tape."

Looking surprised, delighted, angered, hurt on cue without a visible opponent is a challenge, and many trained actors don't like doing that kind of work, although it can pay very well. They prefer to be in a scene with a real, flesh and blood antagonist. It's one reason why many successful screen actors will head to Broadway for a limited run in a play or musical, even if it means taking a pay cut. Others participate in indie films for a pittance of what they would earn in a blockbuster movie. Bruce Willis, Chris Noth, Lizzy Caplan, Chris O'Dowd, and Ron Perlman, for example, all signed up for *Frankie Go Boom*, a hilarious shaggy dog story (with a pig) about sibling rivalry (well worth checking out). Indies usually can't afford the tech budget for fancy special effects and exotic locations and have to rely on old-fashioned screenwriting and storytelling—scenes with repartee between real characters. For actors, that means more interesting roles and dialogue.

But let's get back to the "Pinch-Ouch" method. If you can react with an immediate "ouch" to whatever messages others direct at you—verbal and non-verbal, positive and negative—you have all the talent an actor needs to succeed.

The approach works best with realistic plays and film scripts in which responses naturally fall into realms similar to the ones most of us occupy in life.

It gets tricky when the material you're given, the lines a playwright or screenwriter has penned, don't come "trippingly on the tongue." Eugene O'Neill was a clunky writer with something of a tin ear but great ideas, stories and characters early on (he got better in his late plays.) Making his language sound natural and believable while going "ouch" isn't easy. Shakespeare, Ibsen, Chekhov and some of the plays of David Mamet and Sam Shepard also require more than actors merely reacting to one another.

The first Off-Broadway premiere of Shepard's *True West* at the Public Theater was a disaster. It opened at the end of December of 1980 amid rumors of ongoing trouble. The director had gotten fired, and the playwright disavowed the production. The critics panned it, blaming Shepard's script, and the play closed after three weeks. But they changed their mind two years later when the Steppenwolf Theatre Company, with Shepard's approval, brought its Chicago production of *True West* to New York's Chery Lane Theater. It starred two, then relatively unknown actors, John Malkovich and Gary Sinise, who'd figured out how to use the words to make the vicious comedy of sibling rivalry work and convey Shepard's unique take on America. The play ran for 762 performances.

I saw a production of *Hamlet* at the American Shakespeare Theater in Stratford, Connecticut, staged by Peter Coe, in which Christopher Walken played the melancholy Dane with a monotone Brooklyn accent, mumbling many of the lines. In all fairness, with one exception, no one else in the cast did much better because it had been badly directed. You could tell because every actor was in a different world. Roy Dotrice who doubled as Polonius and the gravedigger laid on the upper crust and cockney accents with a trowel. The young actress playing Ophelia was hopelessly lost and stumbled around the stage as if permanently trapped in her mad scene. Anne Baxter as Gertrude had sprained her ankle before opening—we found that out from a pre-curtain announcement— but, like a trooper, she went on anyway, earning her the affection of the audience and getting a pass from the critics.

Fred Gwynne as Claudius came off best—few know that the man who played Herman Munster on television and did a delicious turn as the Southern judge in *My Cousin Vinnie* was also a Shakespeare trained actor.

Walking out of this disaster, in which the performers had all covered their asses as best they knew how, I overheard a woman in conversation with her teenage son.

"I guess that Shakespeare stuff is just too old for me," he complained. "I didn't understand anything they were saying."

To my surprise, the mother said, "I didn't either. But when I saw Nicol Williamson's *Hamlet* in New York last year, I understood every word."

Doing Shakespeare well requires vocal training. In a 1984 Royal Shakespeare Company production of *Richard III,* Antony Sher played the hunchbacked monarch with two crutches attached to his arms, allowing him to scuttle across the stage like a spider. A gifted young actor, he'd had little vocal training until then and nearly lost his voice by opening night because of the demands of the role—except for Hamlet, Richard III has the most lines of any Shakespeare character. With the help of Cicely Berry, the legendary voice coach of the RSC, he managed to regain his form and won the Laurence Olivier Award for his performance.

I had the good fortune to work with Cicely some years later on a production of *A Child's Christmas in Wales* at Playmaker's Rep in Chapel Hill, North Carolina. A diminutive, feisty woman, she chain-smoked and wore turquoise sneakers—this was long before colorful sportswear became popular. And she was brilliant at getting the young, mostly graduate student cast to relax. During one rehearsal, she took us into the theater, had the actors position themselves up and down the semicircular, tiered seating, and "throw" lines from the play to each other vocally, one at a time. It was a verbal "pinch-ouch" workout that encouraged greater volume and connection across space. With such simple physical games and exercises, and a few adjustments in the pronunciation of certain vowels, Cicely had everyone loosen up and sound convincingly Welsh in no time.

Some intuitive actors figure things out on their own. Stanislavski in *An Actor Prepares* describes how his company was lost for weeks trying to fathom how to do their first Chekhov play before they stumbled upon the keys that unlocked his writings for the stage—subtext and paying attention to the inner, psychological aspects of his characters. Their discoveries and Stanislavski's development of a system of naturalistic acting have made it possible for later generations to achieve similar results in a much shorter rehearsal period.

That's what good training is for. Scene work in acting classes can help you explore how to approach playwrights like Shaw, who needs to be acted in paragraphs, or Chekhov, who works indirectly, with subtext. Or Shakespeare whose language demands heightened energy and many more impulses (pinch-ouches) than a realistic play, not to mention an understanding of how verse works, as well as the vocal apparatus to perform it—articulation, wider vocal range, and stamina. Judy Dench, Joan Plowright, Maggie Smith and Eileen Atkins in the wonderful film *Tea with the Dames* talk about what is required to realize the Bard's works and worry that overly realistic approaches with lots of pauses and "uhs" between words will deprive us of the experience of Shakespeare's larger-than-life poetic theater.

Pinch-Ouch may be the underpinning to good acting, but a performance requires more. It's like building a beautiful edifice. You need good foundations before you can add the support beams, walls, rafters, ceilings and roof, not to mention the decorative elements appropriate to the architectural style.

DON'T PLAY THE END
AT THE BEGINNING

Some actors will read a play or scene and realize it ends badly for their character—imprisonment, embarrassment, death. They come to rehearsal, wearing their knowledge like a raincoat and act like a cloud is hanging over their head. They're anticipating the outcome, and it informs every moment of their performance.

You can't do a play or scene that way. It's too one-note. There is no drama in it, no striving, no struggle, no change.

Losing sight of what's going on can happen to directors, too. During my second time participating in the story adaptation workshop at the Yale School of Drama, I teamed up with Bennett Cohen, an experienced playwright, and dramaturg Rusty Coppenger. The one-act play, *Not Even Killer*, was an adaptation of O'Henry's story, "The Ransom of Red Chief." Our cast consisted of Cordelia Gonzales, Laila Robins and Bill Cohen. Everything went smoothly throughout rehearsals.

Frank Torok came for a late run-through to see what we had accomplished, shortly before we were to present the play to the rest of the school. We were all quite pleased with what we had done, but afterward, Frank huddled out of earshot from the actors with the production team—the playwright, the dramaturg and me—and said, "What happened here? You're in trouble. It just drags on and on."

Taken aback, I asked what we could do to remedy the situation. Frank said, "Speed it up." Which is what we did—problem solved!

Exploring each moment to the fullest, we had lost perspective and had rehearsed the play into the ground. Applying the first part of the old acting formula for success in comedy—faster, louder, funnier—took care of it.

Most actors don't realize when they're playing the end for a whole scene. It's an unconscious reaction, which usually goes away when someone, like the director, points it out to them. Amateurs may have a harder time because they haven't learned yet how to go moment-to-moment. You have to start as if unaware of what will happen and still believe you have a fighting chance every single time you perform the role.

Which raises an interesting point. To act that way requires a certain ability to operate in denial. Fortunately, nearly everyone has that capacity. We are, as far as I know, the only sentient creatures that understand that we're going to die. But we don't live with that realization continually gnawing at the forefront of our mind. We manage to ignore it most of the time and get on with our lives.

Teenagers think they're invincible and that they'll live forever. A severe medical crisis may give them pause or slow them down for a spell, but upon recovery, most quickly become amnesiacs regarding their mortality.

By the time we get into our golden years, even if we're still reasonably healthy, we know each breath could be our last. John Cleese, a member of *Monte Python*, now close to 80, makes jokes about it. We certainly become aware of the limitations of our bodies—slower reaction times, less strength and stamina, longer recovery periods after an injury or surgery—even though we may still feel like teenagers inside.

Even then, most of us don't act morose in the face of our impending death.

This is a good thing.

The best way to achieve some sense of serenity is to stay in the moment. The whole mindfulness movement seeks to teach people how to do that.

Actors have a leg up on the process. It's part of their craft.

Staying curious, focusing on others and one's surroundings, using physical activities to deal with nerves and stress, maintaining an active, positive attitude are all theater techniques whose practice can help make life bearable and enjoyable for the rest of us as well. What we engaged in naturally as children can serve us well toward the end of our life, too.

THE 80/20 RULE
GETTING AWAY WITH IT

I've written at length about my take on the 80/20 rule in another book, *How to Mess with Others for their Own Good*. Basically, it contends that in any walk of life, profession, art or craft, 80% of the practitioners are mediocre. Only 20% are above average (thank you, Yogi Berra, for the math). It's a difficult concept to swallow—especially when you discover you're among the 80% crowd in your chosen field and your bruised ego rebels—but it can be quite liberating when you truly "get it."

In theater or film, that ratio holds true as well. Eight out of 10 actors, designers, writers and directors are mediocre. If you ever hold mass auditions, as I did for a production of Lillian Helman's play, *Another Part of the Forest*, at Equity Library Theater in NYC, where I saw 100 actors a day, five days in a row, you know what I'm talking about. In movies, there are lots of workmanlike directors, but only a handful of filmmakers—from Alfred Hitchcock, David Lean, Orson Welles and George Stevens to Christopher Nolan, Steven Soderbergh and Guillermo del Toro—who tell a visual story through the medium, not just put scenes up on their feet and hope their cinematographer will make them look good.

There is another aspect of the 80/20 rule that is important for the theater profession. If you perform at an 80% level onstage, most audiences think you're giving your all. That's not true in film. The camera is less forgiving, but you only need to get it right once, and few directors are as obsessive as Stanley Kubrick who demanded 74 takes for a scene in *A Clockwork Orange*. But 80% is a good round number for onstage success.

Phew!

No one, not the best or most dedicated actors can perform at full tilt night after night. Too many distractions and external circumstances can get in the way. Maybe you ate something that doesn't agree with you, or you've had a row with your significant other, or you've gotten great news about landing a movie role just before you go on, and the adrenalin pumping through you throws off your timing and concentration.

When I worked at Florida Studio Theatre in Sarasota, Richard Hopkins, the artistic director, and I would watch opening night from a small landing on the left side of the house where the stairs led up to the back rows. We were too nervous to sit in the audience. I am happy to report that, in my time there, we never had a disastrous show. But whether it was a respectable performance or great opening night, as the spectators rose to their feet and started to applaud—in Sarasota, the older audiences love to give standing ovations…because they still can—Richard would grin in relief and say, "Got away with another one."

He understood that you didn't have to be brilliant to satisfy an audience—80% will do. He also believed that much behavior in the theater, including the tremendous amount of energy actors pour into performance, is due to the desperate desire to avoid embarrassment and humiliation. Still, "getting away with it" is often as good as it gets.

That doesn't mean you should just phone in your performance.

I reviewed Ted Tally's play *Terra Nova* at the Yale Rep. A powerful Man Versus Nature drama, it deals with Robert Falcon Scott's doomed 1912 expedition to reach the South Pole ahead of his rival,

Roald Amundsen. When Scott and his men got there, they found the Norwegian flag planted in the snow. Despite all their efforts, they'd come in second. On their way back, they also lost the battle against the weather—blinding blizzards—and a dwindling food supply. Scott is best remembered for his Victorian stoicism in the face of death. He titled his last letter to his wife "To my widow." His journal concludes, "Last entry. For God's sake look after our people."

Tally's play is an exciting, theatrical, moving depiction of human folly, British arrogance and hopeless struggle against extreme conditions. It is not easy on the actors. They have to pull a sled across the stage and spend most of the play wearing heavy fur coats under the merciless stage lights.

I went to see the play again late in the run, and things had deteriorated. At one point, the explorers had to cross a crevasse, a deep chasm in a glacier. On opening night, the actors mimed the action convincingly by leaping across the "abyss" and pulling the sled after them. But after six weeks of performances, they no longer cared and walked right past the gap as if it wasn't there and didn't matter.

If the director had been around to see the show, he would have gone backstage afterward and given them a note, "Guys, put the crevasse back in play."

Keeping a performance fresh is part of an actor's job. Sometimes, specific memories or associations that make a moment possible, especially those requiring big emotions, wear out and no longer trigger the behavior needed. At that point, you have to search for new ways that will get the required results.

When performances get stale, sometimes the stage manager will call for a brush-up rehearsal to tighten blocking that has become sloppy or to get the cast to pick up cues. That is especially important on Broadway, where some shows run for years, and keeping up the quality (at least at 80%) for audiences that pay big bucks for tickets is critical. During the run of the musical *42nd Street*—nine years and 3,486 performances—the producer, David Merrick, and his assistant would go to see the show every few months or so and take notes on which actors still worked hard and which were going through the motions. The latter found themselves replaced, permanently, by their understudies or new hires.

I always pity people listening to motivational speakers who tell them to deliver 110% or more. Not only is it mathematically impossible, putting out 100% is difficult and exceedingly rare.

No one can go full throttle at all times without burning out. Better to do your best and be happy when you manage 80% and get away with it.

MASTERY

My second year at the Yale School of Drama, I took a class taught by film director George Roy Hill about adapting novels to the screen. He was editing *The World According to Garp* at the time, and it was fascinating to hear him talk about how he decided to tell the story of John Irving's hero as a young, developing author in a visual way. The process of writing is notoriously dull on film—you can show someone banging away at a typewriter or tapping a laptop or iPad only for so long. George came up with the ingenious idea to convey the creative evolution in a little cartoon, which was amusing and clever and worked quite well.

What didn't work was how he dealt with the main character's journey from his teens to middle age. George had considered using two different actors but, in the end, opted for Robin Williams to play Garp at all stages of his life. Unfortunately, Williams was too old by then to convince as a teenager.

At some point, George told about the time he directed *A Little Romance*, a sweet film about two precocious teenagers in Paris who run away from their parents (the young girl was played by Diane Lane in her first movie role). The kids want to go to Venice and kiss under the Bridge of Sighs when the evening bells are ringing all over the city. Along the way, they receive help from a charming, old con man played by Laurence Olivier.

Even for the successful director of *The Sting* and *Butch Cassidy and the Sundance Kid*, working with "the greatest actor of the century" was a bit daunting. So, on their first day on the set together, George decided to take a collaborative approach.

"Well, Larry?" he said—everyone in show business called the great Sir Laurence Olivier that. "How shall we do this scene?"

Olivier looked at him and said, "Well, George, I can do this scene a hundred different ways. Why don't you tell me which will work best for you?" It was a gracious way of letting George know, "You're the director. You can tell me what you want me to do."

It also was a sign of the confidence Olivier felt in his skills as an actor. By then he was a master of his craft.

Mastery can occur in many walks of life—photography, gardening, quilting, teaching. I knew I reached that level as an editor when I looked at the paragraph of a novice writer and realized I could say it more succinctly, more clearly, more elegantly, and in five different ways.

It requires time to achieve mastery. In performance art, which is rooted in the human body—acting, dancing, etc. —it takes about 10 to 15 years.

The public often confuses mastery and genius, thinking of the latter as a state of being, a result rather than a process. While it is true that mastery can yield some extraordinary outcomes, few people understand what it takes to get there.

In my first-year scene class, there were two actors, both a bit older, who had come with the expectation that after three years at YSD they would have a methodology that they could apply to solve any role. Both dropped out midway through the first year, frustrated that they weren't getting the "paint-by-the-numbers" approach they were looking for.

Mastery for actors, as a result of years of practice and experience, comes when they have an understanding of how they work—what they need to do to create a role. At the same time, it means having the confidence that they can solve any challenge that crops up along the way, to come up with something suitable and interesting in the three weeks of rehearsal before opening a play, or in the few days to get ready to shoot a movie scene or television episode.

When I directed my first professional production at *Winterfest*, we all attended each other's initial readthroughs. One of the four selections was *Playing in Local Bands*, a comedy by Nancy Fales Garrett about the encounter between a hipster poet from the 1960s and the punk teenager who may or may not be his daughter. Michael Murphy, who played the supposed father, was a 40-something actor with a number of movies to his credit, including *An Unmarried Woman*, *The Year of Living Dangerously*, and Woody Allen's *Manhattan* (a film I loathed when I first saw it. For all its critical kudos, it is essentially a self-serving portrait of a man in midlife crisis conducting an exploitative relationship with a young woman).

In the second act of Nancy's play, Michael's character had a tearful breakdown. When it came to that point in the first readthrough, Michael stopped and said, "I won't cry today, but I'll be ready by the time we open." He was confident that he would figure out how to produce tears when it counted. I know most people think actors will cry at the drop of a hat, and some can, but others have to work at it. Michael understood his craft well enough, trusting that he would be ready; and he was. Offstage, he was personable and generous as well.

Many actors who have achieved mastery can tell you a good deal about what they do to create a performance. For a great example, look at the chapter "Circumstances" in *Respect for Acting*, by Uta Hagen, in which she shares her workbook for Edward Albee's play *Who's Afraid of about Virginia Woolf*. (She was Martha in the original Broadway production and received a Tony Award for her performance).

Jessica Tandy was a wonderful stage actress who had a long career in theater and the movies (you can see her in an important supporting role in Alfred Hitchcock's *The Birds*). In 1989, at age 80, she won an Academy Award for her starring role in the film version of *Driving Miss Daisy*. Seven years earlier, in her last Broadway appearance, she had played Annie Nation, a 79-year-old Appalachian matriarch in *Foxfire*.

What knocked audiences' socks off was a moment early in Act II when Annie flashes back 62 years to the time her husband first courted her. Jessica leapt in the air and in a few dance steps transformed into a young teenage girl. It seemed like spontaneous stage magic. Yet, if you asked her how she did it, as one of my directing teachers had the opportunity to do, she could tell you exactly what created that moment for her—a complex nexus of physical and emotional associations—so she could repeat it night after night. Mastery by a great artist!

Of course, achieving mastery doesn't mean you should rest on your laurels. On the contrary, most people who get to that stage are eager to take on new challenges, roles and projects that will allow them to use parts of themselves as never before. Think of Judy Dench, considered one of England's great theater actors, who took on the role of M in seven James Bond movies late in her career and, as of this writing, is involved in five film projects at age 85.

This a big lesson for the rest of us. So many people stop growing as adults unless life forces them to look farther afield. Sometimes a crisis, like a health issue, loss of a job or a natural disaster, requires them to pick up the pieces and make significant changes. But why wait for an emergency or catastrophe? Why not continue to be curious after high school and college, and keep discovering new possibilities for the rest of your life?

INTERLUDE

HOW GOOD IS MERYL STREEP REALLY?

Is Meryl Streep a great actress?

If you like acting with a capital A, unquestionably. If you prefer acting that seems like you're watching a living, flesh and blood human being, probably not.

The question has its entertainment value even if it is a bit silly, like the arguments sports fans have over who is a greater basketball player, Michael Jordan or LeBron James; or who would win a series between the 1980s Boston Celtics or Los Angeles Lakers and the 2017 Golden State Warriors.

When I attended the Yale School of Drama, the question of Meryl Streep's acting chops came up in discussions in and out of classes with surprising frequency. Remember the dubious reputation of Yale actors—couldn't walk, couldn't talk.... Meryl, with her seemingly effortless ability to master accents and her meteoric rise, first in the New York theater world and then in Hollywood, changed that. (Except for her unconvincing Aussie accent in *A Cry in the Dark*. People in Oz still make fun of her for that.)

Meryl already had several highly touted films to her credit, *The Deer Hunter* and *The French Lieutenant's Woman*, and had earned her first Academy Award for *Kramer vs. Kramer*. Faculty members who knew her from her time at the drama school referred to her wryly as "Our Meryl," although there was considerable pride behind the ironic stance.

But it begged the questions regarding her success. Was it genuine or primarily due to the PR machine that kicked in early and anointed her as the greatest actress of our time? Are the many awards and accolades she has received over the years a recognition of legitimate greatness or overblown hype?

Actually, the question regarding the talent of "our Meryl" has historical roots going back to the debates about who was better—Sarah Bernhardt or Eleanor Duse, Laurence Olivier or Marlon Brando. Or, what is the best way to create a character—from the outside in or inside out? Or, which acting style is superior—presentational or representational.

The last two are rather academic terms, which often create more confusion than clarity. Sometimes, they refer to acting styles; sometimes, they describe the relationship between actors and the audience—are the characters behind a "fourth wall" as if the spectators aren't there, or do they address the viewers directly in asides and soliloquies. I prefer Uta Hagen's terms, "realistic" and "formalistic" for the two approaches. Whichever set one uses, they do stand for an important difference.

On the realistic side are actors who "live the role" both in rehearsal and performance like an actual person. They use various techniques to connect to their character and to have real feelings and real thoughts when they are onstage. In rehearsal, they explore touchstones and trigger points that allow them to repeat their performances yet have a seemingly genuine experience every time. Whatever their process, they don't so much "act" the character as "become" the character.

Formalistic actors may do the same in rehearsals to make discoveries about their roles, utilizing different emotional techniques to layer their performances. They may start "from the outside in" by using physical features such as a limp and, later on, employ makeup and prosthetics to create an appropriate mask. By the time they get to performance, however, they select the moments they think best express their characters. Ultimately, they act their ideas of who the character is and how he or she behaves.

In practice, there is considerable overlap between the two approaches. Some plays demand it. Soliloquies and asides addressed to the audience in Shakespeare and in some contemporary plays are not "realistic" by nature. Certain dramas require different acting styles—Harold Pinter's plays of quiet menace, expressionist drama like August Strindberg's *The Ghost Sonata*, and musicals in which characters burst into song and dance. Actors participating in a farce need to be precise in their actions. The cactus plant in *Noises Off* must be placed in the exact spot every time so that the gag of the egotistical stage director accidentally sitting on it pays off. That requires a more conscious, deliberate approach to performance than living the role like a flesh and blood human being.

It is possible for actors to switch from one approach to the other in the course of a single performance. I witnessed such a transformation—uncalled for—in John Heller's *No Trains for Harris*, which I directed for the inaugural season of the Philadelphia Festival for New Plays. The one-act play is a marvelous farce about a New York corporate executive who has a visionary experience during a vacation trip to the South Dakota Badlands. Believing that he is the reincarnation of a Native American chief, he decides to give up his Wall Street job, camps out in his Upper East Side apartment and meditates on his roots. Whenever his wife tries to reason with him, he declaims a famous speech by Sitting Bull, Red Cloud, Chief Joseph or other tribal leader. In desperation, she asks his boss, Willis, to come and do an intervention. Comic chaos ensues.

Richard Davidson played Willis as a cartoonish, corporate CEO—smooth, glib, and smarmy—the villain of the piece. The contrast between him and the more realistic Harris was very funny. Audiences roared with laughter.

In one performance, however, the spectators included a number of the theater's corporate donors—attorneys, bank executives and high powered businessmen—the kind of people who, if they were Harris' boss, would fire him on the spot. As soon as Richard came onstage in his fancy three-piece suit, acting arrogant and superficial, you could feel them pull back. They felt mocked and didn't like it. Richard sensing their hostility instantly shifted to a realistic approach, presenting a more rounded, caring, identifiably human Willis. And the suits in the audience relaxed and enjoyed the show.

Many actors, especially those with good training, can work both formalistically and realistically, and in combination of the two. But for the sake of understanding, let's take a look at the approaches separately, in their more extreme manifestations.

Formalistic actors like Meryl Streep and Laurence Olivier enjoy putting on accents, prosthetics and other paraphernalia to alter their appearance and help them construct their characters. They like to hide themselves in their roles.

By the way, Hollywood rewards actresses who distort their beauty, using wigs, makeup and masks, with Academy Award nominations and Oscars. Nicole Kidman wearing a fake nose as Virginia Woolf in *The Hours*, Elizabeth Taylor letting her hair go wild in *Who's Afraid of Virginia Woolf*, Charlize Theron uglifying herself in *Monster*, Anne Hathaway dirtied and with hair shorn in *Les Miserables*, and Meryl Streep made up as a jowly Margaret Thatcher in *The Iron Lady*, all received Academy Awards for their performances. Obvious, recognizable, visual expressions of characters are (mis)taken for great acting, even when the actual performances are less than stellar.

You can always tell formalistic actors by the transparency of the choices their characters make, because they have decided on them ahead of time and play the results. You can understand what they are doing at every moment and appreciate the performance. That is why critics and many spectators love them and heap praises upon them.

Formalistic actors are also "safe." In general, they don't make emotional demands on an audience. You will rarely be overwhelmed by unexpected feelings as a result of what they do. A great formalistic actor can wow you but will seldom move you. If you feel stirred, it is more than likely because of what the scene is about rather than the acting. There is always some tension in the performance. The effort of deliberately manufacturing the moment gets in the way.

Watch the famous scene in the Holocaust film, *Sophie's Choice*, when the title character must choose which of her two children to take with her, knowing the one left behind will probably die. Meryl's performance is astonishing in its execution, but you can see exactly what she, the actress, is thinking and doing at the very moment of her harrowing decision.

I met Meryl Streep during the National Playwrights Conference at the O'Neill Theater Center in 1982. She was gracious and lovely, and what I remember most was how natural, soft and likable she was in person, more so than in any movie I'd seen her up to then. Admittedly, she had been cast in roles that didn't demand tenderness, warmth and sensitivity—Linda in *The Deer Hunter*, Joanna in *Kramer vs. Kramer*, and Inga Helms Weiss in the TV mini-series *Holocaust*. *Sophie's Choice* didn't come out until later that year.

Since then, Meryl has gravitated to ice queen roles—Miranda Priestly in *The Devil Wears Prada*, Margaret Thatcher, and Hannah Pitt, the repressed Mormon, in *Angels in America*. On the occasions when she tries to show a tender side, as in *Florence Foster Jenkins* or

The Bridges of Madison County, she "acts" vulnerable, but never "is." Unlike other female performers, she has never moved me to tears; and I usually enjoy watching her male co-stars more—Stanley Tucci, Hugh Grant, Clint Eastwood.

In contrast, with realistic actors, you can't really tell what choices they are making. Their acting seems unpremeditated, spur-of-the-moment. The best display the same spontaneity as animals. (It should come as no surprise that actors hate to perform with animals. Put cats or dogs onstage and they'll command all the attention. Besides the cuteness factor, they are so real you can't take your eyes off them. The other creatures actors loathe having in a scene, for similar reasons, are children.)

Living a role means you're not self-consciously aware of your thoughts and choices. The great British actor Ralph Richardson, after his best performances, was often heard to say to his leading lady, "You were so interesting tonight!" His focus was on the others onstage with him, not on what was going on inside his body or head.

Some film actors have that ability naturally—Marilyn Monroe, James Dean, Robert Mitchum, Jennifer Lawrence. In his video series on film acting, Michael Caine says that when you rehearse on a movie set, it should be as natural as a conversation, and people walking by might join in, not knowing they are stumbling upon a scene in progress. Imagine a whole performance like that.

The emotional impact on audiences is different, too. My third-year directing teacher, Tony Giordano, told me about a time he saw an off-Broadway production—I don't remember which play—that had a superb ensemble cast whose realistic performing was powerful and moving. Walking out of the theater, he overheard a middle-aged woman and her 20-something daughters talk about what they had just seen and experienced. The daughters were enthusiastic, but the mother said, "I hated it. It made me cry."

No doubt she would have preferred more formalistic actors. She would have witnessed and understood what she was supposed to feel and been able to manage her emotions without being surprised by them.

Film is not kind to formalistic actors. While their performances may receive raves at the time, retrospectives don't show them in a favorable light.

Take a look at *The Prince and the Showgirl*, a romantic comedy starring Laurence Olivier and Marilyn Monroe. It is an object lesson in the difference between the two acting approaches. Olivier in his first outing as a director plays the uptight prince of the fictional country, Carpathia. His performance is wooden and stiff. True, his character is a stuffed shirt, but that doesn't excuse the performance being lifeless. In contrast, Monroe as the showgirl is effortlessly spontaneous, sensual, vulnerable, adorable; and she steals the movie. You get why, years after her death, she is still an iconic movie star.

Sometimes a scene in an old film jumps out for its spontaneity and human truthfulness. Take the sequence in George Steven's *The More the Merrier* where Joel McCrae is walking Jean Arthur home and starts to make out with her. When they sit on the stoop in front of her apartment, he keeps touching and kissing her. She tries to fend him off, seemingly resisting his advances, yet responding and wanting more, while talking about the mundane aspects of her daytime office job. It is funny, sexy, and wonderfully alive every time you watch it.

I suspect the formalist approach appeals to actors who don't have the technique to simply be, or who, at some deep-seated level, believe that they won't be interesting enough to others just being themselves. Or perhaps they developed the idea early on that acting requires conscious, effort with a capital E and never learned to do otherwise.

When I assisted Lloyd Richards on a production of Chekhov's *Uncle Vanya*, Glenn Close played Elena, the young trophy wife of the old landowner who comes to visit the rural, backwater estate. A multi-talented actress, she had just finished the musical run of *Barnum* on Broadway and appeared in the film *The World According to Garp*, for which she received an Academy Award nomination.

At the first readthrough, Glenn was Elena—flirtatious, soft, vulnerable and achingly beautiful. Everyone who attended was knocked out by her performance. She was lovely offstage, too, and funny—when, during a break, she got down on all fours and imitated a bucking circus horse, she had the cast gasping with laughter. Gracious and down-to-earth, Glenn reminded me of another New England bred actress, Katherine Hepburn, who never put on airs despite her success and stardom.

In rehearsals, Glenn made many wonderful discoveries in response to other actors, but three days before previews, she started to select aspects of her performance she liked and "acted" them. On opening night and in subsequent performances I attended, she never was as real, spontaneous and compelling as at that first readthrough.

I took notes for Lloyd during tech and previews. At a certain moment, he wanted Glenn to move a foot and a half to the right—it would have created a better stage picture—but he never gave her the direction. Later, when I asked him why he didn't, he said, "It would have thrown her." Then he added, "She has all the talent of a great actress, being able to take in an impulse and respond spontaneously, but she has no technique." He meant that she didn't know how to reproduce the moment spontaneously more than once.

Some actors don't have that technique either yet retain a spur-of-the-moment quality. One of them is Christopher Walken whom I saw in several productions at the Yale Rep both before and during my time at YSD. Always real, like an animal, he presented his fellow actors with a challenge because he never gave the same performance twice. One of the cast members who had played opposite him in Ibsen's *The Wild Duck* told me that it was fun to "rock and roll with Chris." He had the ability and confidence to go with whatever Walken did, but others who expected more consistency onstage had difficulty keeping up.

Years later, Walken was cast in *Catch me if You Can* as the father of con man Frank Abagnale, Jr, played by Leonardo DiCaprio. In an extra on the DVD version, Steven Spielberg describes directing Walken, marveling that he was different in every take, yet completely present. For a film director, that's great. He can select and use the one that works best.

So, what are we to make of the debate of formal vs. realistic acting with "our Meryl"? No question, Meryl Streep is a highly skilled actress. Her choices are complex, layered, and at times surprising and unexpected, yet always germane to the character she plays. They are also perfectly discernible. You can almost watch the wheels turn in her head. If you like that kind of formal approach, Maryl Streep is indisputably its greatest living practitioner. It remains to be seen whether her performances will stand the test of time.

My own tastes gravitate toward the realistic side. I prefer Robert Duvall in *Tender Mercies* to Robert Downey Jr's mannered performances in his *Iron Man* and Sherlock Holmes movies. I think Daniel Day-Lewis is overrated. People are awed when they hear that he stays in character throughout the shooting of a film both on- and off-camera. I suppose he needs to work that way, but it strikes me as a personal quirk, indicating a limited imagination and a lack of technique. For my own part, I don't find his much-lauded performances memorable when I think back on them. Whereas, there are moments of Humphrey Bogart, Spencer Tracy, and more recently, Jeff Daniels, that have stuck with me long after I saw their films.

That is not to say I can't enjoy the other styles of acting from time to time. I like Laurence Olivier at his ham-fisted best. He is a scary Nazi dentist in *Marathon Man* and an over-the-top Jewish Nazi hunter in *The Boys from Brazil*. I love both *Guardians of the Galaxy* movies for Zoe Saldana's green makeup and Chris Pratt's exuberant presence, although I would give best-acting kudos to Groot and Rocket Raccoon (voiced by Vin Diesel and Bradley Cooper). Tatiana Maslany in *Orphan Black* playing and, by Season 2, fully inhabiting more than six very different characters who are all clones, is a marvel of make-up and imaginative technique.

But I prefer Jennifer Lawrence in *Silver Lining Playbook* and *American Hustle* and Rachel Brosnahan in *The Marvelous Mrs. Maisel* and, of course, Helen Mirren, Maggie Smith, and Judy Dench in just about anything they do. For me, it's not about greatness or who's better or best, but who is memorable, whose work is real and honest, and moves me to laughter and tears.

Life isn't about finding yourself.
Life is about creating yourself.

—George Bernard Shaw

ACT III–CAREER ADVICE

MAKING IT PART I—
TALENT, PERSISTENCE AND LUCK

After their productions at the Yale Repertory Theatre opened, many professional directors would come to a special Q and A session with all the drama school directing students. They were open and generous, offering insights into their working processes, and often provided an honest self-critique of their work.

I remember the British director John Madden talking to us about his production of *The Suicide*, a Russian tragicomedy by Nikolai Erdman. I had reviewed John's production of *Measure for Measure* at the Yale Rep a few years back and had liked it very much. (He has since become a successful film director with such hit movies as *Shakespeare in Love, The Best Exotic Marigold Hotel* and *Miss Sloane*). At the seminar, John volunteered that he was at a loss about his most recent effort. Joe Grifasi in the starring role of Victor, a tormented writer, was often brilliant, but he could not hold on to his performance from one night to the next. This was a real problem since Victor was onstage almost the whole time and the play revolved around him. It baffled Madden, and I don't think he ever understood that he had not provided the infrastructure his American-trained actor needed. As a Brit, John was used to actors creating characters on their own and focused on staging, lights and music.

Toward the end of those coffee klatches, invariably one of the third-year students would ask, "Do you have any advice on how to get started as a director?" Usually, we received a canned response about keeping at it and, if you could swing it, assisting someone on an off-Broadway or Broadway production.

The best answer came from my third-year directing teacher, Tony Giordano, after his production of Athol Fugard's *Hello and Goodbye* opened at the Yale Rep. He said, "I can't tell you how to make it. I can only tell you how I made it. Ask a hundred directors and you'll hear a hundred stories. It's different for everyone." Frustrating advice for those of us who wanted a tried-and-true path to success, but honest.

Still, some essential points should be part of any discussion about making it in the theater and movie business, including the well-known trio of keys to success:

- Talent
- Persistence
- Luck

Talent is what you bring to the table. It's inherent. You can't add to it, can't inflate it, can't buy more of it; but you can develop it and hone it.

Some actors are gifted with a fine vocal apparatus. James Earl Jones was chosen to do the voice of Darth Vader in the *Star Wars* movies for a very good reason. His resonant bass-baritone can caress and menace. There is physical beauty you can't buy—Paul Newman, George Clooney, a young Brad Pitt, Elizabeth Taylor, Charlize Theron and Halle Berry all have it. On the other hand, working to enhance your gifts, can pay off handsomely. Cary Grant, a very good-looking man, was an acrobat by training and practiced walking in a casual, elegant way until he became the embodiment of debonair sex appeal.

Some actors touted as young leading heartthrobs don't get their rightful due until middle age when their true talent as character men emerges. When Jeremy Irons portrayed Klaus von Bulow in *Reversal of Fortune*, he showed an unexpected side of his personality to the world and redeemed what was until then considered a "disappointing" career. Ralph Fiennes, although always a bit of an odd duck, appeared in leading man roles in romantic films like *The English Patient* and *Maid in Manhattan*, but he didn't come into his own until cast as Voldemort in the Harry Potter movies. Or take Matthew McConaughey. How much more interesting he has become since playing quirky, eccentric characters in films like *The Wolf of Wall Street* and *Dallas Buyer's Club* than when he appeared on the cover of *People Magazine* as "The Sexiest Man Alive."

So, don't worry too much about how talented you are. Talent is the least important of the keys to success.

Persistence is another matter.

John Houseman, the legendary actor, producer and director, who worked with Orson Welles at the Mercury Theater and was one of the founders of Juilliard and The Acting Company, had a long and varied career. But he didn't become financially successful until his late 70s after landing the role of the crusty old Harvard law professor in the film and television versions of *The Paper Chase*. That led to national commercials for Smith Barney (now Morgan Stanley Wealth Management) and allowed him to make serious money for the first time in his life.

Commenting on being a very late bloomer, he would tell people in his gravelly voice, "If you stay in the theater long enough, everything you want will happen."

I applied to the Yale School of Drama school twice before I got in. It took a director in the class after me six times. Turns out, the admissions committee faculty members looked favorably on candidates who came back year after year, taking it as a sign of doggedness and commitment.

F. Murray Abraham was 45 when he won the Best Actor Oscar for his portrayal of Salieri in *Amadeus*. He'd started out as an actor in New York in 1960 and bounced around doing minor roles until he finally struck gold 24 years later. Dustin Hoffman was 30 and had played bit parts in Los Angeles and New York for a decade when Mike Nichols cast him as the lead in *The Graduate*.

There are plenty of other stories about how staying in the game ultimately led to success. The point is, if you give up too quickly, if rejection crushes your spirit, the theater and movie industry are not for you. If you are a sensitive soul, be sure to develop a tough hide so you can keep going in the face of adversity.

Luck is another thing you can't manufacture.

The theater and movie gods smile on you or they don't, although Louis B. Mayer, the film producer and founder of MGM, famously said, "The harder I work, the luckier I get."

Be that as it may, luck is not something to count on, but you can encourage it to come to you. The best way I know how is to be uncompromisingly clear about what you want. Figure out your heart's desire and own it. This isn't some silly hogwash like *The Secret*, engaging in positive self-talk or imagining yourself already successful. It's about determining what you really want. For actors, this should come easy. They look for it in every role—what does the character covet, passionately? Once you've cracked that riddle, let everyone know about it, and pursue it with every ounce of energy you've got.

When I was a high school teacher in the mid-1970s, I knew after two-and-a-half years in the classroom that my heart wasn't in it. But I had not admitted to myself what I wanted to do instead. I was writing for *The New Haven Advocate*, reviewing productions at the Yale Rep and the American Shakespeare Theater in Stratford, Connecticut. On several occasions after seeing a so-so performance, I said to myself, "I can do better than that."

One night I was sitting in the kitchen of my apartment with my friend Susan Holohan. I was feeling down and kept complaining about how unhappy I was as a teacher and lamenting my lack of alternative prospects. At some point she asked, "What do you really want to do?" and before I could think, I blurted out, "I want to direct plays."

There it was, lying on the kitchen table like a gauntlet thrown down to challenge me. I couldn't take it back, couldn't act like I'd never said it, couldn't insist I was taken out of context or misquoted. I could either own it or ignore it and act as if it didn't matter to me. I decided to pick up the gauntlet.

I knew I'd have to transition into a new career, and the only way I could imagine doing so was to go back to school. Since I lived in New Haven and had developed roots there, I wasn't ready to leave yet and applied only to the Yale School of Drama. I didn't get in, so the next year I applied to four theater schools determined, if I got rejected by them, to apply to eight or 10 the following year.

In the meantime, I read books on acting and directing, and joined the *New England Radio Comedy Half Hour*. Written by my friend James Wimsatt, a multi-talented artist with a gift for comedy and rock and roll, it was an homage to the antics of *The Goon Show* and *Fireside Theater*. We had a lot of fun doing different characters in weird voices. I contributed a film noir episode called *Esmeralda's Mystery*, a pun fest of epic proportions. And I kept writing theater and film reviews.

One afternoon after I'd panned Brustein's production of *The Seagull*, I got a telephone call from Edward Reveaux. He liked my review and wanted to meet me for lunch. An energetic septuagenarian, he wore a patch over his right eye with dramatic flair. He had been a Broadway musical director in the late 1940s and early 1950s and run theaters in Ohio and New Mexico. Now, in the autumn of his life, he still kept his hand in creative work, writing speeches for the CEOs of Volkswagen and Mercedes Benz in Germany.

Ed and I took to each other right away. We were both opinionated and saw eye to eye on a lot of things, from the glories and woes of German culture to the misery of bad, high-concept theater—all dressed up and no place to go! At some point, Ed asked me about my future plans and I mentioned wanting to become a theater director.

To make a long story short, he ended up writing the recommendation that got me into YSD. He also cleaned up my personal statement for the application, giving it focus and pizzazz. Like many shy, artistic wannabes, I had aspirations but wasn't comfortable yet to beat my own drum.

It turned out that Ed was a graduate of the drama school himself. Because he had lost his eye in a freak accident at an early age, he could not serve in World War II; so he pitched in for the faculty members that did, became interim dean and kept the school going during the war years.

I didn't realize how much weight he still carried there until Frank Torok, who conducted the admission interview for directing, pulled the recommendation from a folder and, squinting over his reading glasses, asked me how I knew Ed Reveaux. He was clearly impressed. Perhaps there was a phone call from Ed behind the scenes, too. In any case, I got in.

The point of the story is: If I hadn't known exactly what I wanted, Ed and I would have had a pleasant lunch, perhaps even a follow-up meeting, but my desire to direct plays would never have been part of the conversation and set things in motion.

There is a Buddhist saying: When the student is ready the teacher will appear. Well, the same goes for careers and other goals. When you're really ready, genuinely ready, the most amazing people will pop out of the woodwork to help.

That's how I see luck. You make your own by being decisive about what you want.

MAKING IT—PART II
TO THINE OWN SELF BE TRUE

Actors have big egos, which is a good thing (even though many are also painfully shy). In a profession that comes with a lot of rejection, you have to believe in yourself against all odds. A big dose of self-confidence is essential.

Besides, the business isn't fair. Some fine, talented actors never make it big in the movies because the camera doesn't like them enough. Yes, the camera needs to love you if you want to be a film star, as many wonderful stage actors hoping for a big Hollywood career have found out to their chagrin: Judith Ivey, Alan Howard, George Grizzard, to name a few (and why you probably haven't heard of them).

On the other hand, there are genuine superstars whose acting talent doesn't match their celebrity: Tom Cruise, Harrison Ford, Steve McQueen, Raquel Welsh, Arnold Schwarzenegger, Samuel Jackson, to name a few.

Then there are stars with considerable range who would never be as compelling onstage—Cary Grant, George Clooney, and Reese Witherspoon, among others. Robert Mitchum flirted with doing the title role in *Macbeth* from time to time but always got cold feet. He probably knew he needed more than his animal presence on screen to play the murderous thane onstage. He also had a wry attitude about the profession, famously saying, "I have two acting styles: with and without a horse."

Some are both, fine actors and genuine movie stars—Marilyn Monroe, Robert Duvall, Al Pacino, Robert De Niro. A few become good actors over time: Clint Eastwood comes to mind. But they all have one thing in common: They were and are—to use an old-fashioned term—photogenic.

Still, most actors dream about their Oscar acceptance speech, and many indulge in delusions of grandeur. A lot of them think they can do everything, even if they have played supporting roles for much of their career. Get them plied with enough Scotch or Bourbon and they'll tell you they would make a great Hamlet if only given a chance. Michael Moriarity, best known for playing the assistant district attorney in the first four seasons of *Law & Order*, once let on to an interviewer, and he wasn't kidding, that his dream was to perform *Hamlet* chained to a prison floor and playing all the parts—an astonishing flight of egomaniacal fancy.

A few actors, however, have the good sense to know who they are from early on. They are not confused about their strengths and limitations and what they can and can't do. They know their type for Hollywood.

One of them was John Turturro, an actor in my year at drama school. Equally adept at comedy and serious work, John became a stalwart in Adam Sandler's movies. My favorites are his delicious turn as the butler in *Mr. Deeds* and his over-the-top performance as the Arab terrorist in *You Don't Mess with the Zohan*. As Agent Simmons, he livened up the human side in the early Transformer movies; his performance as attorney John Stone in HBO's *The Night Of* is nuanced and memorable. In his recent film with Julianne Moore, *Gloria Bell*, he is sensitive and likable.

During his final year as a student, John selected two unusual scenes for the League Auditions in New York. In those days, graduating students from Juilliard and the Yale School of Drama had the opportunity to perform two scenes before an audience of casting agents, producers, and other members of the entertainment industry to give them a leg up in their fledgling careers.

John understood that, as an Italian kid from Brooklyn with something of an overbite, he was not likely to become a famous Shakespeare actor. In the second-year verse production of *The Winter's Tale*, he'd been cast as the Old Shepherd, a prose role.

When it came time to prepare for the Leagues, John chose one scene from David Mamet's *Edgar* in which the eponymous anti-hero chokes his date for the evening to death when she refuses to acknowledge that she is a waitress, not an actress. The other was from *Total Eclipse* by Christopher Hampton, in which Arthur Rimbaud gets into an argument with his fellow French poet, Paul Verlaine, and plunges a knife into his hand.

When John presented the scenes to our third-year acting class and the acting department faculty, the teachers were aghast. The League attendees would be turned off by the violence. John would cripple his career before it had a chance to get off the ground. At best, he'd be typecast as a villain for the rest of his life. They strongly urged him to reconsider, but John stuck to his guns (and knife) and performed both scenes at the Leagues.

He was the first actor in our class to get work in movies and television. He has since become a talented writer and film director as well, mining his roots for his subjects. As a character actor, he has played a wide range of roles and appeared in the Coen brothers' *The Big Lebowski* and *O Brother, Where Art Thou*, and starred in *Barton Fink*.

John also displayed persistence early in his career. He originated the title role in John Patrick Shanley's *Danny and the Deep Blue Sea* at the Humana Festival in Louisville, Kentucky. The play is a funny, brutal, and ultimately redeeming encounter between two lost strangers, "bar-crossed lovers" who help each other recover their humanity. When it moved to the Circle in the Square Theater in New York, the playwright wanted a more established, "name" actor, but John fought for the role and received rave notices for his visceral performance. The *New York Times* critic Mel Gussow marveled, "Even as a poet in the rough, he retains a savage, animalistic air, so much so that it is a surprise to learn that he is a trained actor and a 1983 graduate of the Yale School of Drama." As though training would turn a good actor into a tamed beast!

The point is that John knew how he would be seen, both at the League auditions and in his early career, and he was okay with that. He also had no trouble distinguishing between fantasy and reality. While he chose two violent scenes to highlight his talent, he is a sweetheart of a man. Above all, John knew his type, or at least what would give him entry into the film industry. He wasn't a leading man or matinee idol, but a heavy like Humphrey Bogart, James Cagney, Edward G. Robinson, and James Gandolfini, who all became memorable stars and got to play good guys after a while, too, because they were so compelling.

The lesson here is Socratic: Know thyself. Or, at least, keep working at it. We live longer now than we did 100 years ago. Why not use some of that time to discover what we're made of and what we're really good at?

MAKING IT—PART III
DON'T FAKE IT TILL YOU MAKE IT

The recommendation to court success by "faking it" has jumped like a wildfire from the theater world to the rest of society. It has become a favorite cliché in the presentations of many a motivational speaker.

But it is bad, cynical advice.

That doesn't mean you have to study and achieve perfection before hitting the road to stardom or whatever success you're chasing. Just do your best at all stages of your journey, and if you can exude confidence along the way, so much the better. Some will argue that is as good a definition of "faking it" as any. They don't understand the essence of performance, which always contains big "what ifs." They also fail to realize that pursuing a career has to honor the process as much as the results.

A significant part of that process means doing work on yourself. You should take the time—daily if possible, certainly more than once a week—to reflect on your situation in life. There's nothing wrong with sitting still, engaging in a little navel-gazing, and contemplating who you are. Again, the Socratic advice: Know thyself.

I know it's considered un-American to do that. We prefer to spring into action, "damn the torpedoes, full steam ahead." But without self-knowledge and a degree of comfort in your own skin, nothing you do and accomplish will ultimately come to good. You will screw up your marriage and your kids, tank your friendships and, in the long run, cause yourself physical and mental harm.

Many creative people come from dysfunctional family backgrounds, grow up in divorced households, or suffer the death of a parent at an early age. The many interviews James Lipton conducted as host of *Inside the Actor's Studio* with actors, directors, writers and comedians speak volumes about their emotional scars.

What many people don't get is that psychic wounds don't just inhabit the mind but become part of the body. How we carry ourselves relates to our mental state. Chronic back pain, headaches, diverticulosis, hips and knees that need to be replaced earlier than expected are often the bitter harvest of poor lifestyle choices and emotional trauma, unheeded for too long. When we are young, the body compensates and absorbs a good deal of psychic punishment without showing any obvious signs. But as we get older, it has less flexibility to contain the damage. By the time people get to their 50s and 60s, it will exact its pound of flesh, to be Shakespearean about it.

Faking it till you make is an attitude that gets in the way of developing an authentic self. Even if you hit the jackpot, part of you will feel like a fraud and you won't enjoy your triumphs. If you don't work on yourself and just keep chasing success, you won't be happy when you get it because it won't satisfy the needs that have been driving you all along. You won't feel like you've earned it and will use negative, destructive means to fill the void inside you.

No wonder that medicating physical and psychic pain has reached epidemic proportions in our society, especially in the abuse of opioids (the fact that they are physically addictive as well make it worse). It's why the Betty Ford Clinic in California never lacks patients seeking to cure their drug dependencies. And why so many people who seem to have it all, commit suicide—John Belushi, Heath Ledger, Whitney Houston, Philip Seymour Hoffman, Robin Williams and, more recently, Anthony Bourdain and fashion designer Kate Spade. The accolades they received for their talent and well-deserved success never touched or appeased their demons, never helped heal their deeper, psychic wounds, never made them whole.

Life is more complex and layered than fame and fortune. That is why you need to keep working on yourself to achieve balance and learn to enjoy yourself while pursuing your work, goals and dreams.

Faking it till you make it will never let you do that.

ALWAYS SAY YES!

John Houseman used to give young actors a piece of advice, based on his more than 60 years of experience in the theater and film industry: "Always say Yes!"

If you're offered a job, say Yes! If it is a small role not incompatible with your ego, say Yes! Even if it's an insipid television ad, say Yes! (Especially to a national commercial—if successful, the residuals will keep you well-fed for years. Think Flo in the Progressive ads.)

If the play or movie requires you to do things that might make you uncomfortable, say Yes! Elizabeth Taylor hated to wear a silky slip in *Butterfield 8*, but she did it and won her first best actress Oscar in 1961 (in spite of her eight marriages, she was a rather proper and conventional—and material—girl).

I met a number of young actors who proudly proclaimed, "I will never take my clothes off, play an evil character, or do a politically incorrect role." They wanted to stay true to their values—no nudity, no violence, no torture like in the *Saw* movies, no characters that would make them look ugly. But when you pound the pavement starting out, your qualms and self-imposed standards, however good they might make you feel, are not helpful.

Better to put your personal ethics, politics and religion in your pocket and instead of worrying whether to bare or not to bare, always say Yes! Relish the opportunity to explore the more uncomfortable, unattractive aspects of humanity—dark dreams, silly or embarrassing behavior, rampant sexuality, murder and mayhem.

Isn't that what you signed up for in the first place, the ability to act out wicked fantasies with impunity? People who require safe spaces and want to root out micro-aggressions need not apply. The theater life is not for them.

So, short of a role asking you to do something truly repulsive, unforgivable or racist, or having to endure sexual harassment as a condition of getting the job, always say Yes!

The reason to do so, Houseman explained, is that if you start to cherry-pick your roles early on when the one comes along that you really want, guess who will get it? The actor who always said Yes!

The theater and film industry are relatively small ponds, and word gets around about who can be counted on. Plus, you never know who might come to see your show and remember you favorably.

I directed a summer stock production of Emlyn William's *Night Must Fall* in Rhinebeck, New York. The play is an old chestnut, a murder mystery in which a charming young hustler kills an old woman and receives his comeuppance. I was offered $150 and room and board for three weeks' work. I could have turned up my nose, but I didn't.

We rehearsed on a make-shift stage in the back of a barn that had been converted into a theater and performed inside. It was an enjoyable experience both on and offstage. The cast and I went to see movies together on our days off and sat at picnic tables after spaghetti dinners, drinking wine and reading poetry to each other by candlelight.

The following year, I was hired to direct Martin Epstein's *The Man Who Killed the Buddha* at the New Theater of Brooklyn (TNT). The parable play tells the story of Kenji, a naive, young monk looking to achieve Nirvana, whose guru gives him the job of polishing the statue of the Buddha in the courtyard of the monastery. Kenji does so for 20 years, resisting all kinds of monetary and sexual temptations and becomes something of a holy man, attracting pilgrims from far and wide. The avaricious guru charges admission for visitors to watch him polish. When the Buddha finally appears, laughing uproariously at his disciple, Kenji realizes that he has wasted his life, kills the Buddha and leaves the monastery for good. The play is funny, poetic, filled with visual surprises, puppets and stage magic. Despite its title and lessons, it will trouble only insecure Buddhists.

Geoffrey Owens played Kenji, projecting innocence and ambitious charm with a gleam in his eyes. While we were in rehearsals, he got an audition for *The Cosby Show* and was cast in the role of Elvin Tibideaux, the boyfriend and subsequently, husband of Sondra Huxtable (Sabrina Le Beauf). He recently made news headlines for working at Trader Joe's to support his family awhile pursuing his career in the entertainment business. Considering the wide variety of grunt work many actors do on their way to "making it," the job-shaming he received was pernicious, ageist and stupid. To his credit, Geoffrey weathered the storm with grace and good humor.

TNT's enterprising artistic director, Deborah Pope, offered an exciting fare of new plays. Some of them were avant-garde and attracted prominent artists, including Susan Sontag and Linda Hunt. I had been talking with Deborah about directing at her theater for several months. One of the reasons she wanted to engage me was that a TNT board member on her summer vacation had stopped for a night in Rhinebeck, seen my production of *Night Must Fall*, liked it, and remembered it favorably when my name came up.

As Fats Waller liked to say, "One never knows, do one?"

Many actors will say No to a role if they think the play is not very good. They worry that appearing in a turkey will reflect badly on them. That's a mistake. It simply isn't true that a bad show will hurt you, although a good production with lots of critical acclaim can propel a career forward, allowing cast members to ride its coattails to success. Otherwise Emma Stone, whose performances I have liked in movies like *Easy A* and *The Help*, would not have won the best actress Golden Globe and Oscar for *La-La Land*. She couldn't dance, couldn't sing, and wasn't even all that interesting in the role of Mia, an aspiring actress.

But appearing in a crappy show will not damage your career. Just look at Gene Hackman and Michael Caine. They always have said Yes! even to schlock movies, so long as they got paid, and they've always acquitted themselves well. When Caine was asked about his appearance in *Jaws IV*, he famously said, "I have never seen it but, by all accounts, it is terrible. However, I have seen the house that it built and it is terrific."

In my second year at the Yale School of Drama, my directing teacher, David Hammond, invited me to see the musical *Lock Up Your Daughters* at the Goodspeed Opera House. The show is about a 17th-century highwayman-rake and his amorous exploits. A former student of David's from A.C.T. was in the production and had asked him to come. I was happy to tag along. We got off the train in Old Lyme, where the young actor was waiting with a borrowed car. As he drove us up the Connecticut River to the house he shared with other cast members, he kept apologizing for the terrible production we were about to see.

He was right. It was worse than he claimed—ineptly staged and poorly paced. In the love duet, the director had isolated the two principles on opposite sides of the proscenium, making it impossible for them to interact directly and fix the number on their own. (Many actors keep working on a show during the performance run and improve what they couldn't solve in rehearsals.)

But what I recall most was the spirited performances every one of the cast members gave. Their talent came through loud and clear, despite the poor production. We assured our host that he and the other actors were okay. Any casting director or agent who happened to see the show would remember them favorably.

Always say Yes! and do the work to the best of your ability, and you'll be fine.

That goes for the rest of life, too.

LEARN HOW TO SAY NO

My second year at the Yale School of Drama, I assisted director David Jones in a production of *Rip Van Winkle*. Written by Richard Nelson, the epic play had a huge cast, including some third-year drama school students. David, a Brit with a prominent bald head—this was before the follically challenged hairstyle became popular for men—had achieved success at the Royal Shakespeare Company in Stratford, England, and was about to direct the film version of Harold Pinter's *Betrayal*.

He was great at staging big crowds and choreographing complex scenes, like the knock-down-drag-out fight between Rip and his shrewish wife, which involved breaking a lot of kitchenware. David made it look ugly and dangerous while ensuring that the performers were always safe. Working from behind a desk, where he kept a bowl of jelly beans for the actors to come and take, a subtle way of nurturing while asking for obeisance, he was like a general marshaling his troops. But he wasn't good at helping actors with their performance—the drama school students in the cast were frustrated because he hardly paid them any attention. Again the British expectation that they would create their characters on their own.

As a large-scale drama set in the Hudson River Valley in pre-American Revolution times, *Rip Van Winkle* required a host of period costumes. Jane Greenwood, who was a professor of design at the drama school, oversaw the Yale Rep's costume department and supported Gene K. Lakin, the costume designer for the production. She had already garnered Broadway credits, including Richard Burton's *Hamlet*, as well as the films *The Four Seasons* and *Arthur*—the first one with Dudley Moore and John Gielgud. Since then she has won numerous awards and was inducted into the American Theater Hall of Fame in 2003.

In my encounters with her, Jane was personable, helpful, knowledgeable and sharp as a needle. I learned from her comments to Catherine Zuber, who did the costumes for my thesis project, *The Bewitched*, that it's a designer's job to tell the story of the play through the costumes, but not to draw unnecessary attention to them. For the clothes of the main characters you have to play it straight, but with minor roles and walk-ons, you can let your imagination run riot…up to a point.

For some reasons, Jane and David didn't get along. The first time they had an argument, David asserted his directorial prerogative and put his foot down. After that, he never had a chance. Whenever he asked for something Jane didn't want to provide, she became a ditz. She'd go all fluttery and daft until he threw up his hands in frustration and walked away.

Jane's performances were as impressive as they were calculated. I knew they were put on because, at one point in the middle of acting scatter-brained with David, she winked at me. She knew exactly what she was doing to get her way without saying No directly!

I used her non-confrontational approach in my own way the following year when I was directing *The Bewitched*. The play is a roaring farce about the last Austrian Habsburg monarch on the Spanish throne. By the time Carlos II became king, inbreeding in the imperial family had debased the royal line to the point that he couldn't chew solid food, suffered from epilepsy and was impotent. In many of the play's hilarious scenes, everyone in his entourage, from church prelates to nobles to washerwomen and court jesters, is trying to get Carlos to have an erection and somehow impregnate his German queen to keep the dynasty going. They even hold an auto-da-fé, hoping that the spectacle of heretics burning at the stake will arouse the king. As a take on the grotesque lunacy perpetrated by the enablers of hereditary monarchy—and by implication, anyone colluding to support an inept, egocentric leader in a position of power and authority, no matter how unfit—the play is outrageous, viciously satirical and hysterically funny.

I was fortunate to have a stellar cast. John Turturro played Motilla, the scheming Dominican priest. I will never forget his hilarious, larger-than-life monologue, during which Motilla has himself flagellated and keeps shouting at the novice monk to whip him harder—harder!—until the poor acolyte faints from exhaustion. Roc Dutton portrayed his Jesuit counterpart, the devious Cardinal-Archbishop Pontocarrero, dressed in a crimson cassock, with unabashed ruthlessness. Angela Bassett as Beatriz, the treacherous queen mother, was wonderfully schizophrenic. She alternately argued with Joey, her pet parrot and alter-ego, and became him, squawking and beating her arms like wings, until she finally wrung his neck. Bill Kux as Carlos, the hapless king, cavorted ape-like around the stage, often teetering on the brink of falling down. In one scene, tired of his Royal Dancing Master pointing out that he was less than nimble-footed, he ordered his court to imitate him and together they did a wacky, herky-jerky dance that ended with them all toppling over sideways. When the dancing master objected, "…but 'er, 'tisn't the 'Pavan,'" Bill, as the delighted monarch, crowed, "No, 'tis 'The Carlos.'"

I discovered early on in rehearsals that Barnes was a genuine dramatist who had imagined the action in three dimensions. Once the actors understood what was going on, many scenes and sequences virtually staged themselves. There was one scene, however, that kept giving me trouble. It took place in a palace chamber where the king was holding an audience. As Barnes had written it, balloons were to drop from the ceiling so a furious Carlos could stomp around and pop them like a petulant toddler. It seemed an unnecessary gimmick, and I didn't ask for them in the initial budgeting process, trying to save some money to use on other, more spectacular effects—like the giant phallus the queen rides at the climax of the auto-da-fé at the end of Act I.

No matter what I tried, the scene refused to work in rehearsal. At some point, it occurred to me that Barnes had added the balloons to cover a writing problem. While important information was being related, it just wasn't funny enough on its own. It definitely needed help. Carlos popping balloons in a childish temper tantrum was just the thing to delight and distract the audience.

But when I asked for balloons during the next production meeting, the technical director (TD), also a third-year student, balked. They hadn't been budgeted for. There was no more money. I would just have to do without.

I was stunned and furious, but rather than throw a hissy fit that would have gotten me nowhere, I said, "Ok, let me think about it."

In the next two production meetings, the TD kept trying to get me to agree that the balloons were officially nixed. But rather than say No and cause a fight, I kept postponing making the decision.

By then I had tried the scene with balloons in rehearsal and— voila!—it worked like a charm. I had to have them.

So, my set designer, Dereck McLane, and I went to work behind the scenes. Dereck had done productions with Peter Sellers, the theater and opera director, when they were undergraduates at Harvard, and he was always game for productive mischief. He has gone on to a great career, designing Broadway and television productions, winning

Tony and Emmy Awards and, since 2013, creating the sets for the Academy Awards ceremonies.

We bought balloons, sneaked into the theater in the dead of night, and rigged a simple drop in a suitable spot among the light battens high above the stage. When we tried it out, the colorful balloons descended to the floor as merrily and festive as at the close of a political convention!

The next day, we presented the drop to the TD as a fait accompli. He gnashed his teeth but agreed to let us use it, provided we took care of it on our own, paying for the balloons and rigging them ourselves. We were happy to oblige. It needed to happen only six times—for the tech rehearsal, dress rehearsal and the four performances—so Dereck, the stage manager, Linda-Jo Greenberg, and I blew up balloons and put them up in the drop before every show.

After we opened, the TD took me aside and apologized for having been such a hard-ass. He said it had come on order from the head of the tech department who insisted that his students had to learn to resist the "whims of directors" or they'd be driven crazy. It's a small-minded, overcontrolling approach for a performance art form. Theater requires creativity and flexibility by everyone involved.

The lesson is: Learn to say No without getting into a big confrontation. The work always comes first. If you don't let your ego get in the way and persevere, more likely than not the situation will resolve itself in your favor.

In the inimitable words of the Rolling Stones—ASCAP is adamant about enforcing copyright laws for lyrics—so I will paraphrase, "You may not always obtain what you desire, but if you keep making the attempt…sometimes…you'll get away with it!"

Brush up your Shakespeare
Start quoting him now.

—Cole Porter, *Kiss Me Kate*

INTERLUDE

THINGS GO BETTER WITH SHAKESPEARE!

BANG!

That's how *The Tempest* starts, with an ear-shattering thunder-clap during a raging storm. *Romeo and Juliette* has a street brawl early on between the servants of the rival Montague and Capulet families that turns into a battle royal. Macbeth opens with three witches stirring up toil and trouble. And in the first scene of *Hamlet*, the hero encounters the ghost of his father on the wind-swept ramparts of Elsinore Castle.

The reason for these bloody, bold and resolute beginnings was that Shakespeare had to contend with an unruly crowd of noisy spectators milling about in the confines of the Globe Theater. He knew from experience that he had to get their attention before they would listen to his words. So, he devised openings that would shock them into silence—for his audiences, the appearance of witches and ghosts was an exciting if frightful event. In short, the Bard knew how to make an entrance.

Hollywood filmmakers have imitated Shakespeare's approach for years. No one who has seen the opening of the first Indiana Jones movie on the big screen will ever forget Harrison Ford running from the giant boulder rolling after him. After such a nerve-racking beginning, you know you're in for a great ride!

Every James Bond movie starts with a mini-caper—a chase, a gun battle, a clever infiltration of a secret enemy compound that gets blown up in a fireball. And Disney's *The Lion King* opens with a spectacular musical number in which the newborn lion cub Simba receives the homage of all the members of the animal kingdom.

But Shakespeare didn't just invent attention-grabbing openings. He had the melancholy clown, Jacques, in *As You Like It* proclaim that, "All the world's a stage," and then he brought all the world onto his stage. The Bard's plays jump cut from ocean-faring ships to hillside castles, from enchanted isles to English meadows and forests, from French and British battlefields to brothels, royal bedchambers and lowly peasant huts. Shakespeare hopped around Europe and the Mediterranean in time and space—Syracuse, ancient Rome, Alexandria, Tyre (in modern-day Turkey), Bohemia, Venice, Padua, Verona, Sicily and Denmark—like a tour guide on a whirlwind cruise.

American musicals came into their own when their book writers opened up their stories to the world in the same manner. *My Fair Lady*, based on *Pygmalion*, a single-set play by George Bernard Shaw, travels to many locations, including a London street, a Victorian drawing room, the races at Epsom Downs, and more. Soliloquies offered models for songs that reveal a character's desires—"Wouldn't It Be Loverly"—and reflections on their situations—"I've Grown Accustomed to Her Face."

Shakespeare enriched our language like no other writer, coining words and phrases with abandon—bedazzled, fashionable, manager, new-fangled, pageantry, with bated breath, in a pickle, and cold comfort, to name a few—and abandoned many of them after using them only once, including kicky-wicky, slugabed, and incarnadine.

He could be bawdy and romantic, philosophical and poetic, rabble-rousing and soothing. He wrote fine curses—"I'll beat thee, but I would infect my hands," (*Titus Andronicus*). "Thine face is not worth sun burning," (*Henry V*)—penned popular song lyrics and knew better than anyone how to turn a catchy phrase.

Add to that Shakespeare's uncanny ability to give insight into the souls of all kinds of people and imbue them with humanity—kings and queens, menials (tradespeople), soldiers, lovers, jesters and mountebanks. Even a stock villain character like Shylock in *The Merchant of Venice*, a depiction many now consider anti-Semitic, has moments of eloquence to evoke our compassion ("If you prick us, do we not bleed?"). Shakespeare understood the vagaries of the human heart and was able to convey them better than any of his contemporaries and most writers that came before and after him.

No wonder the Bard of Avon is a man for all seasons. Like the Bible, his works contain multitudes and bountiful advice for all occasions.

Need a comment on baseball? "Foul is fair and fair is foul" (*Macbeth*), and "A hit, a palpable hit!" (*Hamlet*).

Want to know why the most unlikely couples shack up? "Love is blind" (*The Two Gentlemen of Verona*). Although he didn't come up with that notion, Shakespeare was the first to enshrine and popularize the phrase.

Bad jokes? "Knock, knock. Who's there?" (*Macbeth*).

Self-help? "To thine own self be true" (*Hamlet*). "Love all, trust a few, do wrong to none" (*All's Well That Ends Well*). "There is a tide in the affairs of men, which taken at the flood, leads on to fortune" (*Julius Caesar*).

So, brush up your Shakespeare in all of his guises and expressions. It is an investment that will pay dividends far beyond the confines of the stage.

*An average director directs. A good director
leads and follows at the same time.*

—Kensington Gore

ACT IV–DIRECTING

THROW CAUTION TO THE WIND

During the spring of my first year at the Yale School of Drama, I assisted third-year director Jim Simpson on his thesis production of *Benten Kozô*, a 19th-century Kabuki play by the Japanese dramatist Kawatake Mokuami. The title character is an outlaw, and he and his band of four thieves, pilfer the countryside using skulduggery and disguises. Their shenanigans lead to swordfights, chases and other exciting adventures. In the end, after a furious battle, the police surround the gang, and each thief reveals his true identity in a stirring monologue. Benten Kozô himself commits seppuku—ritual suicide—to atone for his crimes.

Kabuki is a highly stylized form of Japanese theater and *Benten Kozô* is considered one of the best examples—think Samurai movies laced with Jackie Chan-like physical comedy and the tragic end of *Crouching Tiger, Hidden Dragon*. It requires bold visual storytelling, with colorful costumes, movable scenery and other theatrical effects, like undulating blue cloth and flats cut out to look like waves for river crossings. A ramp, called *hanamichi*, runs from the proscenium along the left side of the audience to bring the action closer and allow for more exciting chase scenes.

Clever sight gags abound. I recall Kate Burton, dressed in a fat suit that made her look like a giant sumo wrestler, playing a colossus who created an earthquake wherever she walked. This was before she made a career of strait-laced, professional women and conservative politicians like Vice President Sally Langston in *Scandal*. Whenever Kate stomped on the ground, everyone else onstage jumped up in unison, giving the impression that the earth was bucking under their feet.

In another memorable Kabuki convention, actors punctuate important lines with a signature pose called a *mie* (pronounced "mee-ay"). This elaborate dramatic gesture utilizes the full body and extreme facial expressions to create a picture of heightened emotion—fury, passion, sadness, joy, disgust—and reveal the essence of a character. The actor holds the position for a moment, like a statue, and then gets on with the scene.

I still chuckle when I think of Reg E. Cathey, who played one of the outlaws, performing his "cocaine" *mie*. He rose on one foot, ran his nose along his forearm, screwed up his face and struck a pose of quixotic bliss. Reg E. appeared on television in *The Wire* and won an Emmy for Outstanding Guest Actor in a Drama Series for his portrayal of Freddy Hayes in Netflix's *House of Cards*. It's a shame he died when he was only 59 years old.

Jim Simpson chose *Benten Kozô* because he was something of a renegade himself. He liked to ride his motorcycle to New York, braving the traffic on the Connecticut Turnpike, and he embraced the outsider role of being a holdover from the Brustein era in the Richards administration with gusto. But he also knew how to form a close-knit company. The faculty had been lukewarm when Jim proposed *Benten Kozô*—they considered it comic book theater rather than a serious play—and he had fought tooth and nail to get it approved. With most of the actors in the cast belonging to the third-year, lost generation, Jim created an "us vs. them" narrative to unite the cast—"them" being the new drama school administration and "us," the band of rebels, paralleling the play's story of lovable bandits thumbing their noses at authority.

Having been a child actor—he appeared in two episodes of the original television series *Hawaii Five-O*—Jim knew how to make the most of his cast. He kept telling the actors that their greatest strength was their physicality and encouraged their athleticism whenever he could. In that regard, he echoed Stanislavski, who advised young actors to do vaudeville rather than the in-depth, Chekhovian character explorations he was famous for. Of course, Stanislavski was a man of the theater and knew a lot more about process than some of his serious-minded, Method disciples.

Jim also liked to say, "If we manage to be as exciting as a baseball game, we're doing great." You have to put that comment into historical context. In 1977, Reggie Jackson thrilled his fans hitting three home runs in a row, off three first pitches, by three different pitchers, in game six of the NY Yankee's World Series victory over the Los Angeles Dodgers. Two years later, it was amazing to watch slugger Willie Stargell take his team on his back (and bat) and win the World Series for the Pittsburgh Pirates. That happened before football and basketball games became American television's favorite athletic contests. In any case, Jim's point was clear to everyone in the cast—make it as riveting as a sporting event.

The production was madcap, visually thrilling and fun, but the faculty was underwhelmed. The directing critique session afterward became rather testy, with Jim rejecting most judgmental comments as irrelevant. At one of the performances, I had watched four 12-year-old kids shepherded by one of their moms. They loved every moment, laughing and bouncing up and down in excitement. I decided Jim was right and that the faculty members, however, professionally oriented, were a bit too stodgy for their own good.

Fortunately, when David Hammond arrived the next year, he was not. He had been at A.C.T. when that company presented some pretty wild productions, including a commedia dell'arte version of *The Taming of the Shrew* in which muscle man Marc Singer as Petruchio lifted Kate above his head like a dumbbell during the taming scene. It was David who suggested that I do *The Bewitched* for my thesis project.

Assisting Jim benefited me greatly when it was my turn. He showed me how useful and important it is to unite the actors into a coherent company, and the lengths to which you can push the boundaries of conventional theater. I used his *hanamichi* thrusting into the audience from both sides of the proscenium stage in my production. They came into their own in a riotous dance number led by a club-footed court jester to Gershwin's "Clap Yo' Hands" that had the audiences in stitches.

The most important lesson I learned: Throw convention and caution to the wind. The theater permits just about everything. Once you get that and apply it to the rest of your life, irreverence, outrageous comedy and other inspired silliness will become your secret weapons against annoying people who take themselves too seriously; not to mention, bureaucratic rule sticklers, self-centered power-mongers, egomaniacal politicians and all-around yahoos.

KEEP IT SIMPLE

I directed a musical adaptation of a Dylan Thomas short story, *A Child's Christmas in Wales*, at Playmaker's Rep in Chapel Hill, North Carolina. The original tale interweaves Thomas's memories of Yuletide from ages six to twelve. We used a thrust stage made of dark brown planks, empty except for two portable, wooden benches and a wrought iron streetlight to suggest the city of Swansea in the 1920s. Moving the benches around allowed us to create different locations—kitchen, living and dining rooms, and snow-covered streets and playgrounds. We mimed large items of furniture and most props—tables, lamps, plates and cutlery, etc.—to convey a sense of memories in which the characters and events stood out. The only exceptions were essential props like snowballs for a fight and Dylan's favorite Christmas present, a small toy train that choo-chooed around an oval track at the front of the thrust stage to the delight of the audience.

The play centered around an adult Dylan looking back on his childhood and becoming a youngster at different ages from scene to scene. There was also a younger version of him, played by a fifth-grader from one of the local schools, dressed in the same black pants and dark brown, knit sweater. The boy appeared from time to time on the outskirts of the action like a younger memory and witness. In the final moment of the play, the older Dylan, looking back on his childhood, watched him standing in a spotlight as snowflakes drifted around him.

I was fortunate to have Cal Winn play Dylan Thomas. He had extensive experience performing in Shakespeare productions all over the country and handled the Welsh dialect and poetic language with ease. He had done two memorable turns as Falstaff in the *Henry IV* plays, once sporting his own belly when he weighed 180 pounds, and another in a fat suit after he'd slimmed down. He said the second time was more fun and felt liberating.

Cal was a fine actor who could carry a play, which was a good thing since the story revolved around his character and he was onstage the whole time, both as narrator and participant. His tireless and imaginative approach in rehearsals set the tone for the entire company, from the student actors in the graduate training program to the professionals and theater faculty members.

At one point, Cal was costumed in a woolen coat for a snowball fight, and it needed to come off because the play jump cut to the middle of the toasty living room of the Thomas household. I spent a lot of time obsessing, trying to find an elegant way to get his overcoat offstage. I choreographed the young Dylan to come and take it from Cal and added other instances in the play where he could bring him appropriate props.

Cal agreed but looked uncomfortable. When I asked him about it, he said, "It takes the control out of my hands."

I understood immediately. He was right, both from an actor's perspective and for the play. He was the agent of memory; he generated all the action and needed to be in charge. So, I bagged the idea and told him why I'd come up with it—because I couldn't think of a better way to get the damn coat offstage.

He looked at me and said, "I'll take care of it."

The next time we rehearsed the transition, he shrugged off the coat, took a few steps to the left, tossed it offstage, and entered the next scene without missing a beat.

As the "ringmaster" of the event, he could do anything he wanted to and get away with it.

Duh!

I learned three big lessons that day:

Trust your actors and call on them for help when they clearly know what they're doing.

Don't overthink it. The simplest solution is often the best.

And don't beat yourself up over having missed the obvious. It may be staring you in the face, but unless you happen to stare back, you're going to miss it!

WHO'S YOUR DADDY?

Directors have to be good multitaskers. They work with set, costume and lighting designers on the look of the show, and with composers on the music to underscore scenes and transitions. If it's a new play, there are rewrites to incorporate and keep the author stays happy and on track. Above all, the cast members need to become part of a coherent experience, even if they come from different acting traditions and backgrounds, which requires guiding them in their performance. Good directors keep their antennae well-tuned, not just on the progress of the production, but on the company's frame of mind. It helps to make friends with the stage manager who often has a better sense of the backstage mood, rumors and goings-on than the director.

I came to realize fairly early on that, whether I liked it or not, I was not just the leader, but the father of the production. Especially for the actors. This is understandable, given the nerve-racking tension leading up to performing before a live audience and dealing with the fear of embarrassment. Actors, if they're any good at all, don't have perspective on how they come across—focused on their role and their character's actions—and they need feedback from someone they can trust to tell them that what they're doing works. Putting themselves in the hands of a director they haven't worked with before is something of a leap of faith.

Martin LaPlatney, a seasoned actor, director and fight choreographer, once told me what he learned from Paul Giovanni, the

Tony-nominated director and author of *The Crucifer of Blood*: Even the most damaged actor, who has worked with incompetent and mean-spirited directors, still wants to believe that the next one will be better, maybe even special. All you have to do in the first few days is be organized, have some decent knowledge of the play, be kind, and make people feel that their talent and opinions are welcome.

Directors come in many types and personalities and wear the parental mantle in different ways. Some are angry fathers who shout and scream and intimidate actors to get them to do what they want. Others use charm or try to energize their cast through sheer force of personality. Still others find ways to support their cast members both through staging and timely suggestions about characters. Often, the latter have been actors themselves and know what will help or hinder a good performance.

According to Martin (and Paul), it's best not to tell actors what to do or how to do it, even if they don't know Acting 101. Better to give them the sense that you are asking them to do something you believe only they can accomplish. Then, they will give you the very best that their talent permits. Good advice on how to treat people in any profession, to encourage them to do their finest work.

Having a sense of humor helps, too. I was in Atlanta directing *The Provok'd Wife* by John Van Brugh, a Restoration comedy about the battle of the sexes with surprising contemporary resonances. The male lead, Stuart Culpepper, played an older husband who is worried about being cuckolded by his young wife. Stuart was a popular local actor and his voice was well-known to Atlanta audiences because of its resonance and his ability to draw out the word "diamonds" into three syllables—"di-a-monds"—in frequently aired radio commercials for a jewelry store.

When I was casting the play, I went to see him in a production of Eugene O'Neill's *Desire Under the Elms* and offered him the part over drinks afterward. During our conversation, we took each other's measure. He was a good 20 years older than me, and while my Yale Drama School credentials impressed him enough to say yes, I knew I would have to prove myself at some point and pass a further test.

The opportunity came soon enough when Stuart didn't show up for the first rehearsal. The stage manager informed me that he'd been arrested for drunk driving the night before and was in the process of getting out of jail. When he arrived looking sheepish, I waved off his apology, chuckled and said, "I hear you were doing character research for the tavern scene in the play last night." He laughed and we were on best of terms for the rest of our time working together. Stuart was funny, inventive and created a moving portrait of a man who, for all his bluster, found love late in life and knew it was his last chance at happiness.

Sometimes you have to be tough. In *Painting Churches* by Tina Howe at Florida Studio Theatre, Henry J. Quinn, a former FBI agent who had become an actor upon retirement from the bureau, played Gardner, the elderly father. He was quite good and, because of the dearth of older men in theater, got a lot of jobs. In an early rehearsal, I asked him to move to a particular spot onstage the next time we ran the scene. He ignored me and stayed put. When I pointed out, "I asked you to go there," he said, "You never told me that."

I blew up at him and shouted, "I know what I said and I meant it! That's where I want you to go!" It was an instinctive, pinch-ouch reaction on my part. I must have sensed that I had to show him who was boss. I apologized after rehearsal—Henry was old enough to be my father—but I could tell he was actually quite pleased when I "lost it." My outburst told him that I was capable of being in charge, which allowed him to relax and focus on doing his work.

I realize that calling a director the "father" or "mother" of the production is a double-edged metaphor at best. While it suggests that the cast and crew are a family, it also implies that actors are children. That some actors can be petty and childish is undoubtedly true, but so are the rest of us, even those in positions of power and authority (Donald Trump is a prime example). But calling actors children and treating them as such is condescending and denies their unique talents, professional know-how, generosity and work ethic.

In my career as a director, I learned a great deal about theater craft and other matters from actors. I remember a searching, insightful conversation with Cal Winn about the changes in our society. It was triggered by the sense of family life in *A Child's Christmas in Wales*. Cal could relate to the Dylan Thomas story (and play) because he grew up in an extended family himself, where grandparents, aunts and uncles all reinforced the shared values his parents tried to instill. That is no longer the case in an America where so many children are reared in nuclear or single-parent families.

Another time, at a student matinee of the play, when the lights went to black before the show started, the kids in the audience began to laugh nervously and yuk it up in the darkness. Just as I started to worry that Cal wouldn't be able to establish the proper mood for the gentle opening, I heard him roar from the stage, "Quiet!" The audience hushed immediately, the lights went up, and he began Dylan's monologue. Having had plenty of experience with noisy school audiences at the Oregon Shakespeare Festival, Cal was a veteran at dealing with nervous, unruly youngsters.

Sometimes, you have to be that ruthless as a director, too, and do the unexpected. I staged an evening of one-acts that included *Party for Six* by Wolfgang Bauer, an Austrian playwright who was something of an enfant terrible in the 1960s. The play takes place in the hallway of a big city apartment where a wild bash is in progress, with the increasingly intoxicated attendees passing through on their way to and from the bathroom. Their conversations reveal the go-ings-on in the living room and provide a fun, edgy peek at youthful binging on sex, drugs and rock and roll. Things get started with the toilet flushing as one of the party-goers exits the lavatory, setting the scene for the rest of the action.

But on opening night, as the stage lights went up, the toilet didn't flush, leaving the audience clueless as to what was happen-ing—not a good start for a comedy. Watching from the back of the house, I realized I had to do something to avert disaster. I hurried backstage, stopped the show, went out front and addressed the spec-tators, "Unfortunately, we had a technical glitch, and an important sound effect at the beginning didn't happen. It's essential for under-standing to what's going on, so we're going to take it from the top."

There was half-hearted applause, and we started over. This time, the toilet gurgled on cue, eliciting peals of laughter from the audi-ence. The performance got a rousing send-off it never would have received had everything gone according to plan.

As you gain directing experience, you realize that actors work in different ways. How you tailor your response to what they bring to rehearsals can make a big difference.

In one of the second-year acting classes, Roc Dutton brought in a scene from August Strindberg's *Dance of Death*. The play is a dark comedy about a hellish marriage, a frequent topic of the Swedish playwright who knew about the murky side of matrimo-ny from personal experience. Roc played the husband, a retired artillery captain, with a physical handicap not indicated in the script—his left arm hung down from his side like a withered war memento. David Hammond critiqued the scene and praised Roc's apt physical choice. But when he had him and his partner do the scene again, the crippled limb was gone. An intuitive actor, Roc had focused on the action, unaware of what was happening with his arm. Once it was pointed out to him, something in his process no longer clicked, and the behavior disappeared.

In my second-year workshop production, *Lear Dream*, Roc played the title role. We concentrated on the heath sections where the old monarch goes mad, howling at the thunderstorm that mirrors the whirling tempest in his mind. Roc gave himself to Shakespeare's language and made physical discoveries that astonished everyone. In one incantatory speech, he sank to the floor as if trying to conjure and pry open the ground beneath his feet. His 1990s television series, *Roc*, and other screen roles give no sense of how powerful of stature and voice he can be. Knowing his intuitive approach from scene class, I made sure never to comment directly on anything he brought to the character, and his performance was visceral and moving.

Giving notes to actors often requires an indirect approach. It's why directors will convey their suggestions in images, metaphors and stories. In *Uncle Vanya*, there is a scene in which Dr. Astrov, smitten by Elena, shows off a map he's made to document the deterioration of the surrounding countryside. At some point in rehearsals for the Yale Rep production, Lloyd Richards suggested to Harris Yulin, who played Astrov, that it was like taking out his wallet with a stranger he'd met and showing him the pictures of his children. Harris was considerably more energized and passionate the next time through the scene.

Early on in rehearsals of *The Provok'd Wife*, Stuart Culpepper told me that he'd played George, the male lead in *Who's Afraid of Virginia Woolf* in three different productions. The first time he was too young and it was a learning experience. The second time he thought he did okay. But the third time he nailed it when he mapped every moment of George's journey in the play to Verdi's *Requiem*. It sounded far-fetched, but I nodded as if it made perfect sense. From that point on, I included musical terms in my directions to him. When I wanted him to pick up his cues, I'd say, "This moment can be more legato."

I also decided to choreograph the street brawl in the first act to the accompaniment of Wagner's *Ride of the Valkyries*. Stuart was happy because the music helped him stay on track with all the physical business the fight required.

Good directors will use staging and editing creatively to help actors with difficult moments, and not just to compose an attractive stage picture or film frame. When I saw *The Godfather* again during my time at drama school, I noticed that, in the last scene in which a hysterical Connie (Talia Shire) accuses her brother Michael Corleone (Al Pacino) of having had her husband killed, director Francis Ford Coppola showed her mostly from behind as Michael tries to comfort her. It occurred to me that Shire, who was wonderful as the shy Adrian in *Rocky*, wasn't capable of utilizing her lines to reach the distraught emotional state required, so Coppola helped cover her limitations and told the story in quick jump cuts and by focusing on Michael assuming his role as the new godfather. Brilliant!

The indirect approach also works well if you need to help an actor play a king, queen or powerful crime boss: Have everyone else in the scene relate to him or her with fear, respect and obeisance.

The other side of the coin is understanding that a lot happens without you. Directors don't need to be control freaks for a production to thrive. The best keep their eyes and ears peeled for those moments when actors invent on their own, or when their performance takes a sudden leap, and they acknowledge the discoveries by incorporating them into the fabric of the production with gratitude.

FALLING IN LOVE

As a director, when you first notice that your leading man and leading lady have fallen in love on- and offstage, you feel a jolt of anxiety, take a deep breath and hope for the best. What's going on is usually quite transparent, and you can track the stages of the developing relationship in rehearsal—the initial attraction, the mutual excitement, the consummation or, rather, the afterglow the next day. It makes for great chemistry in performance, adding an extra dose of sexual frisson and romantic excitement.

Anyone with eyes in their head watching the movie *To Have and Have Not* can see that Humphrey Bogart and Lauren Bacall have the hots for each other. They met on the set, fell in love, married after Bogart divorced his wife and stayed together for 12 years until his death in 1957.

Actors Susan Greenhill and Martin LaPlatney became a couple when they worked together on a production more than 20 years ago and have been partners ever since. "Martin likes to joke that one of the reasons he got into theater was because it says in the script the girl has to kiss you," Susan told me. "It certainly worked with me, and we're still kissing, even without a script."

When Cupid's arrows hit the target that way, you desperately hope that the honeymoon lasts at least until opening night when the critics come. I once directed a play—I won't say which one—in which the leading actor went to bed with three of the actresses (serially, not all at once). Fortunately for the production, he kept his leading lady for last and their affair didn't end until the show closed.

The problem is that any cooling off in the relationship is just as apparent to onlookers. If the co-stars don't get along for a reason—they break up, one rebuffs the advances of the other, or they don't like each other—it does not bode well for the production. Bruised egos all-too-often make for ice-encrusted performances on opening night.

While love in the theater can be a good thing, in film not all off-screen love affairs guarantee artistic success. The tabloids are full of accounts of the torrid liaisons of movie stars, but becoming a supercouple didn't translate into steamy on-screen chemistry for Ben Affleck and Jennifer Lopez (Bennifer) in *Gigli*, Brad Pitt and Angelina Jolie (Brangelina) in *Mr. and Mrs. Smith*, or Meg Ryan and Russell Crowe in *Proof of Life*.

Of course, great actors will deliver regardless of what happens backstage. A recent book revealed that, during the filming of *Casablanca*, Bogart behaved like an ogre toward Ingrid Bergman on the set. He was going through a rough patch in his marriage—this was before he met Bacall—and he preferred to get drunk and play chess by himself in his trailer rather than have dinner with his Swedish co-star. However, their romantic scenes together betrayed none of that. In fact, they have become iconic examples of two people deeply and hopelessly in love.

A veteran actress told me about being on a national tour in a romantic comedy. The road can be a lonely place and you find comfort where you can. In this case, it was in the arms of her leading man. Hooking up cemented their performance and made the nights after the show more fun. From experience, she knew that the affair would be over when the tour ended. It had happened before and it was no big deal—to her.

Her husband felt otherwise. When he came to see the play, he realized what was going on from watching the performance. When he confronted his wife afterward, she was nonchalant about it, which made it worse. Not being a theater person, he became quite upset. It took considerable effort to convince him that the fling was part of the work, well, sort of, and had nothing to do with her love for him, and to restore balance and harmony to their marriage.

I was propositioned by both female and male actors a number of times in my career. My first job after graduate school was director of a touring company. Before we hit the road, the actors, crew and I went to a bar to get better acquainted. During a game of pool, one of the actresses pressed her breasts against me from behind long enough to make clear it was accidentally on purpose. When I didn't respond, she backed away and acted as if it didn't happen. Not that I wasn't tempted, but I knew it would make being in charge of the company difficult for me, especially if our relationship didn't work out along the way. Two days later she hooked up with one of the other actors for the duration of the tour.

So, what are we to make of the proliferation of love and sex in the arts? Is it that society is more lenient now than in the past, even with the slew of abusive sexual behavior by Harvey Weinstein, Bill Cosby, Jeffrey Epstein and others. Is it because there is more lurid coverage on television, in the tabloids and on the Internet than ever before?

Henry Miller, the writer whose sexually explicit novels were initially banned in the United States in the early 1960s, famously said in the movie *Reds* where he appeared as one of the "witnesses" (interviewees), "You know what I think? That there was just as much fucking then as there is now." He was referring to the scandalous relationship between John Reed, the leftist journalist played by Warren Beatty, and Louise Bryant, played by Diane Keaton, that had tongues wagging in the decade before the Roaring Twenties loosened America's straight-laced morals.

People in the arts have always led unconventional lives and gotten it on with greater frequency than more traditional members of the establishment. That may be less true nowadays since the "free love" movement of the 1960s, although there are reports that millennials are having less sex than previous generations. Still, both high profile couples and ordinary folks don't always get married, even after they have children; and women are no longer forced to wear a scarlet "A" when their adulterous transgressions come to light (except voluntarily, like Emma Stone in the movie *Easy A*).

In the wake of the revelations about sexual predators and abusers, from Bill O'Reilly and Roger Ailes to Harvey Weinstein and other Hollywood's power mongers, the demands of the #MeToo movement will reverberate through American society for years to come. No doubt love and sex will become an even more complicated business in the theater and film industry as a result, but it won't stop people from sleeping with each other.

I can only speculate why so many actors get involved with their co-stars offstage and off-screen. Other than working at close quarters, which can lead to excessive fondness and more, I suspect it happens for three reasons.

One is that people who meet on the set and haven't known each other before genuinely fall in love. That can lead to relationships lasting long after the project is finished and sometimes result in lifelong marriages.

Another is that many actors lack the imagination and, yes, technique, to act it. Love and sex are intimate matters, and while actors tend to examine just about everything they experience to mine it for potential use later on, they don't have enough perspective on themselves to know what turns them on, or what their triggers are for getting romantically involved. Unless they can give their imaginations free rein, they can't fall in love with someone without going to bed with them. I'm not saying it's a conscious thing, but acting it out offstage can make up for lack of acting chops and create the necessary chemistry.

The other side of that coin (and third reason) is that many male actors, especially young leading men, are not yet comfortable with their sexuality. Everybody thinks he's a better than average car driver, but when it comes to sex and love, people may not be as confident. Getting it on offstage takes care of some of their insecurity.

It's why many men and women find that sex after 50 is much better than when they were young. By then, they have let go of performance anxiety and the need to prove themselves, and they can relax with their partners and have a good time.

During the auditions for *Coyote Ugly*, we found two middle-aged actors we liked for the father and mother, Ed Seamon and Dorothy Holland. They had not met before, so to make sure they would work well as a couple, we brought them in together for call-backs (follow-up auditions). By then, they knew what the play was about and their relationship in it. We gave them the scene we wanted them to do, and they looked it over and talked quietly off to one side. When they reached agreement, they got going. Before we could blink, Ed pushed Dorothy up against a wall, kissing her and pulling up her blouse to fondle her breasts, and she responded. It takes a lot of confidence in yourself and your acting to be that free on such short notice.

Often, gay men will make excellent onstage and on-screen lovers for women. Not being sexually attracted to their co-stars gives them the freedom to use their imagination and acting ability to the fullest. At the same time, the lack of sexual tension relaxes their female partners to do their best and the result is great chemistry.

Many male directors fall for their lead actresses. The stories of Alfred Hitchcock's twisted attraction for his blonde, leading ladies—Grace Kelley, Kim Novak, Tippi Hedren—are the stuff of

Hollywood lore. James Cameron's affair with his *Terminator* star, Linda Hamilton, Tony Scott and Brigitte Nielsen during *Beverly Hills Cop II*, and Luc Besson and Mila Jovovich while filming of *The Fifth Element* made for plenty of tabloid fodder.

I can understand why such relationships, either unrequited or consummated, occur. As a director, I always fell in love with the actresses in my cast and, to some degree, with the male actors, as well. Although I am not gay, I could develop an emotional attraction to the men and the characters they played. I have watched other directors fall in love that way, too, and not follow through, preferring to play the role of monk or father abbot to maintain their objectivity and give their actors the freedom to do their work unencumbered.

I made the decision early on not get romantically involved with the actors in my casts, certainly not during rehearsals, tempting though it was at times. I knew I wouldn't be able to handle the fallout if things didn't go well and maintain the necessary detachment to keep guiding the production successfully. After opening, as the glow of my emotional involvement waned, in most cases the attraction faded, too. It had been more about our mutual investment in the play than any real interest in each other. As a freelance director, for much of my career I also left town soon after opening, so that there were no opportunities to follow up and see if anything would develop.

During the production of *The Man Who Killed the Buddha*, I met a talented costume designer. Susan and I have been together for more than 30 years now. Of course, being artists, we couldn't help being unconventional. We had our son Erik first, took him on our honeymoon to Europe as a baby, and got married later that summer. We also worked together on several plays when I was still directing in the theater, and it never affected our relationship away from the productions negatively.

MALICE AFORETHOUGHT

The great British director Tyrone Guthrie—a major regional theater in Minneapolis is named after him—once said, "You must forgive actors everything except malice." He understood that the stress of facing a live audience could lead to rather bizarre behavior. For actors, baring their souls in front of others is fraught with tension, and they deal with the pressure in a variety of ways.

In the production of *No Trains for Harris* I described earlier, the 40-something actor playing Harris had both a wonderful hangdog expression and the vocal power to transform into a Native American chief addressing his tribe. He also threw up before every performance.

At some point, I asked him, "Matthew, why do you put yourself through that?" He answered without hesitation, "Because I love being in front of an audience."

It's what he had to do to cross that line that separated him from the safety of the herd and step out on his own. There is a reason for the much-quoted actors' nightmare—finding themselves alone onstage, usually stark naked, unable to remember their lines. Performing in a play before a live audience is as nerve-wracking as giving a speech in public.

Laurence Olivier had a different way of overcoming that anxiety. In his days, theaters still had thick, heavy curtains at the front of the stage that were raised, drawn or parted when the play began. Olivier would peek through the slit as the spectators settled into their seats and, out of their earshot, heap abuse on them, cursing them with every vulgar oath and expletive he had in his repertory. Being a Shakespearean actor, he knew plenty of salty ones, too. Having worked himself up by unleashing his tirade and given his demons their due, he was ready to perform.

I worked with an actor who, as opening night approached, started to leave various articles of clothing on the set during and after rehearsals—not just costume pieces, mind you, but his own shirts, socks and underwear. The stage manager didn't make a scene. She procured a box and put his personals items in it for him to pick up at the next rehearsal.

In 1984, I assisted director Norman René in the original off-Broadway production of Craig Lucas's *Blue Window*. The play unfolds in three scenes that flow seamlessly into one another, following a group of friends—pre *Sex in the City*, New York singles and couples—before, during and after a party. One of the actresses in the lesbian couple, Christine Estabrook, decided to use me as a lightning rod for her character's anger at men. It was not a pleasant experience to have her glower at me throughout rehearsals, but I knew enough by then not to take it personally. Or rather, I knew it didn't have anything to do with me—I had done or said nothing to her to provoke such relentless ire. After opening, at the cast party, she explained she had done it to help her create her role and apologized;sort of.

No malice, just selfish, self-centered behavior in the name of art. I could understand it but, in all honesty, I was pissed off, and it took me a while to let it go. Christine is a good actress and has had an excellent career since, mostly on television. She played recurring characters in *Desperate Housewives*, in four seasons of *Mad Men*, and in a number of episodes of *American Horror Story*, and I wish I had had the opportunity to work with her again under kinder circumstances.

For my first job after drama school, I became road director for the ANTA Touring Company. It was an off-shoot of the Acting Company, which had been founded in 1972 by John Houseman and Margo Harley to create an apprentice program for talented young actors after they graduated from college. They mounted professional theater productions and toured across America, performing them on college and university campuses. The ANTA Company did the same with high school graduates who had received an Irene Ryan Acting Scholarship award. That program, administered by the Kennedy Center in Washington, DC, had been endowed by Irene Ryan, best remembered for playing the feisty Granny Clampett on television in *The Beverly Hillbillies*.

I assisted directors Christopher Markle and Louis Scheeder to put together two plays and a musical. Then, our motley crew crisscrossed America by bus from New York to Los Angeles, from Moorhead, Minnesota to Key West, Florida. Our accommodations were often fleabag, budget hotels. That led Lisa Kron, one of the actresses on the tour, to quip that ANTA stood for "Actors Nobody Thought About." Lisa had a wicked wit and kept us entertained on the bus for many of the tedious stretches of our odyssey. She has since become a fine playwright as well, winning two Tony Awards for the musical *Fun Home*.

My responsibilities included coordinating with the tech crew, who drove ahead in trucks filled with sets, props and costumes to get them ready at our next performance venue. I also had to keep the shows in good shape, map out the travel itinerary from one gig to the next, and combat boredom on the part of the actors by finding things to do when we had more extended layovers than a day or two. We had a lot of fun doing brush up rehearsals, visiting the San Diego Zoo, and snorkeling in Key West.

On our way from Las Vegas to Gallup, New Mexico, I suggested we take an excursion to see the Grand Canyon. It would have added only two hours to the bus ride, but the actors outvoted me. None had ever been to see that natural wonder, but most of them wanted to get to the Motel 6 as quickly as possible to lounge by the pool and turn on the black and white televisions in their rooms. I couldn't believe it and fumed for most of the ride there. Then I got over it—no malice.

Most people are not devious by nature. They don't go out of their way to upset or hurt you, even if you think they do. That doesn't justify stupid, unkind behavior, even if it happens unawares. You have a right to complain. But don't hold it against the perpetrators for too long.

I understand that it's one thing to forgive or ignore extreme acting-out in the service of a bigger goal—getting a good performance and production, making a decent movie. That's a relatively easy one.

Doing the same in your personal and regular work lives is a bigger challenge. But you have to ask yourself—with a spouse, misbehaving children, or co-workers that drive you crazy—what's really going on? Are they trying to annoy you or do you harm, or are they just being insensitive or troubled themselves? Whatever issues they may have, ask yourself, "Am I overreacting?"

Life is too short to be caught up in a loop of mutual blame or to carry a grudge to the grave. Only malice deserves retaliation.

HIGH CONCEPT

I once saw a production of Shakespeare's *Julius Caesar* set in a banana republic. The actors ran around in khaki military uniforms, brandishing machine guns. Oddly, in the early acts, which take place in Rome, senators were dressed in contemporary, reddish brown robes—a nod toward togas, I suppose.

Of course, the modern-day outfits and props didn't go well with Brutus saying lines like "How ill this taper burns!" while carrying a flashlight instead of a candle. Or when he committed suicide in Act V, ancient Roman style, asking his servant, "Hold thou my swords and turn away thy face while I run upon it." Going with the concept, I had been looking forward to watching him blow his brains out with a Glock.

The evening had one redeeming sequence. There were large television monitors mounted above the stage, and Marc Anthony's famous funeral oration over Caesar's dead body—"Friends, Romans, countrymen…"—was televised in real time as it occurred onstage. It was almost impossible to tear your eyes away and not to watch the speech on the monitors. Just as at a football game, the image on the big screens was more compelling and eclipsed the live action below. It was a perceptive statement about the power of electronic media, but overall the production was an unsatisfying mess.

Another memorable disaster was a production of *King Lear* I attended at the Asolo Theater shortly after I moved to Sarasota, Florida. The director, Megs Booker, had set the play in the Stone Age.

The concept itself was not a bad idea because the harshness and cruelty of the play can work well in a cold, barren winter landscape. The problem was in the execution. The cast was dressed in animal skins and pelts, but except for Doug Jones, who played Gloucester (and had received his training in England), none of the actors took their surroundings seriously. He alone shivered in the cold while the rest looked like they were on vacation in Bermuda—in bear and wolf furs. By the last act, it became clear that the production had exhausted the costume budget, because the pelts yielded to traditional, medieval period gowns and men's clothes made of various fabrics, even during the final scenes on the battlefield.

In retrospect, that event was emblematic of Booker's troubled tenure as Artistic Director. Hired to bring national prominence to the Asolo, she all but ran Florida's largest regional theater into the ground. Having little interest in the community and mounting big-budget productions that flopped, she pursued a ruinous fiscal policy, and two year's later the theater nearly closed its doors. It took the concerted efforts of Managing Director Linda DiGabriele, Associate Artistic Director Bruce Rodgers, Development Director Donna Gerdes, and a few loyal patrons with deep pockets to keep it afloat.

To deal with the Asolo's existential crisis, the board replaced Booker with Howard Millman, one of the founders of the theater—he had been managing director from 1968 to 1980. After that, he successfully helmed other regional theaters, becoming executive director of the Pittsburgh Public Theater and producing director of Geva Theater in Rochester, New York.

Howard returned to Sarasota in 1996 as producing artistic director of the Asolo. He knew the city and theater patrons well. Looking over the donors' lists, he found surprising gaps. "I don't see the names here of five people who would give $10,000 to sponsor a production," he said. "How is that possible?"

To turn things around, Howard expanded the donor base and built bridges with other arts organizations, including FST where I was working at the time. He restored a repertory approach, performing plays in rotation, and invited back into the company popular actors, including Brad Wallace, Dough Jones, David Howard, Isa Thomas and Carolyn Michel, healing the rift with the many spectators who had stayed away.

Once again, knowing one's community and the local audience was critical to success. By the time Howard retired in 2006, the Asolo was on sound financial footing again. To date, he is the only founder of a theater in America who, having left it, was rehired to lead it again. But I digress.

My all-time favorite high concept for Shakespeare came from someone I overheard at a party in New York who wanted to do the War of Roses tetralogy—the three *Henry VI* plays and *Richard III*—in a basketball court, with the Houses of York and Lancaster wearing white and red jerseys, respectively. The audiences would sit in the bleachers on either side. This young genius wasn't kidding!

In movies, high concept usually means the director showing off by using all kinds of clever and weird camera angles, regardless of whether they have anything to do with the story.

Notable examples were the Coen brothers in their early outings—*Blood Simple* and *Raising Arizona*. Critics loved them because it gave them plenty to write about, but that didn't excuse mannered presentations. Fortunately, the Coens have become better cinematic storytellers since—in *Fargo*, *The Big Lebowski*, and *No Country for Old Men*.

Great filmmakers do both, use the screen for visual impact and tell a good story. It's one of the reasons David Lean's *Lawrence of Arabia* and *The Bridge on the River Kwai* remain high on the list of the 100 greatest films. Yes, they have star-studded casts and outstanding performances, but there is also amazing visual storytelling that supports the narrative without distracting. Who can forget the long, wide-angle shot of the flickering desert and Omar Sharif's entrance as Sherif Ali—a distant dot that slowly grows bigger as he approaches riding his camel? To get the full impact, you have to watch it in a movie theater on a big, wide screen.

That doesn't mean realism is the only way to go.

Take Alfred Hitchcock's *Vertigo*, in which the weird, disjointed camera angles reflect the deteriorating mental state of the detective played by Jimmy Stewart.

I've seen excellent concept productions in the theater, too. Romanian Director Andrei Serban's evocative version of Strindberg's *The Ghost Sonata* at the Yale Rep with Tony Shalhoub and Max Wright was a feast of expressionist acting and staging. Lloyd Richards directed Ibsen's *Hedda Gabler* on a set painted a lurid red, furniture and all. He took the idea from a famous Swedish production by Ingmar Bergman. While the performances were naturalistic, the crimson surroundings, in a nod to Sigmund Freud, were a powerful theatrical setting for the psychological drama enacted by the play's desperate, neurotic and ultimately doomed, female protagonist.

If you're going to do a concept production, you have to work it through and make sure your actors are on board with it too. I remember the presentation Peter Wallace gave to our directing class at Yale for his thesis production of Calderón's *Life is a Dream*. The 17th-century Spanish drama deals with the conflict between free will and fate when a king convinces his rebellious son that all his agitating was just a dream. Peter explained that he would do the play in period costumes but add contemporary elements, like the protagonist brandishing a revolver, to give it a sense of hallucinatory dislocation.

The faculty raised objections: it wouldn't make any sense and confuse the spectators. Peter ignored them. For the set, he had his designer, Rick Butler, create a black-and-white checkered ramp, curved and twisted like a nightmarish M.C. Escher dreamscape, with a bank of mirror panels along the back for surprise entrances. There were just enough contemporary touches to suggest a surreal fantasy world. At the critique following the performances, everyone agreed that the concept had worked.

Notice, none of this has to do with the people watching the performance. It's all about a director's vision and approach. But ultimately it is the audience that determines whether or not the concept works.

A director friend told me about the time he staged a production of Alan Ayckbourn's *How the Other Half Loves* at his summer stock theater in Pennsylvania. The play concerns three couples whose lives are hopelessly and hilariously intertwined, and it has a marvelous gimmick: All the action takes place in two houses superimposed on the same set, like two separate realities conflated. Actors appear in both places simultaneously, their dialogue overlapping as they walk through the action of one scene while engaged in the other.

The Midwestern audiences were baffled. The director tried every theatrical trick he knew to clue them in on what was happening—including swiveling chairs at the dining table—turned to the left, they indicated sitting in one room; turned to the right, in the other. He had alternating, different colored panels installed on the back wall of the set—to no avail. The audiences never got the concept, and the production was a failure.

Just because these spectators were not as sophisticated or theater savvy as big city audiences didn't make them rubes. It's a matter of experience and exposure. In Sarasota at Florida Studio Theatre, Richard Hopkins has built the largest subscription audience of any theater its size in the country, not by "dumbing things down" but by using talk-backs, newsletters and extensive program notes to educate his spectators for the more demanding shows. He also schedules plenty of comedies and musicals, popular with Midwestern audiences. Like Lloyd Richards when he took over the Yale Rep, he understood early on that, as a producer, he has to keep an eye out for who walks through the theater doors and can't just do art for art's sake.

I had my own, amusing experience with one dissenting audience member during my Yale Summer Cabaret season when I directed Bertolt Brecht's didactic one-act, *The Exception and the Rule*. The play tells the story of a merchant who ruthlessly drives his servants and carriers through the Gobi Desert in a race against the clock to clinch an important oil deal. When the caravan gets lost in the scorching heat, one of the servants approaches the merchant with a water can to offer him a drink. The merchant thinks it's a weapon and shoots him. During his trial for murder, the judge finds that the servant's gesture of compassion represented the exception—most underlings would not have given their hard-driving boss a life-saving drink. The rule is that a servant would take revenge, and the merchant was well within his rights to defend himself and is therefore acquitted.

As a play about misperception, fear and racism, *The Exception and the Rule* is surprisingly contemporary. Considering the chokehold killing of Eric Garner and shootings by police of unarmed black men, including Michael Brown, Alton Sterling and Sam DuBose, and the exoneration by white judges and grand juries of the police officers despite testimony by witnesses and even video evidence that the men killed were unarmed, things haven't changed all that much since the play premiered in 1930. The convictions for murder of Jason Van Dyke, the Chicago police officer who killed 17-year-old Laquan McDonald in 2014, and Dallas cop Amber Guyger, who fatally shot an unarmed Botham Jean in his apartment, are big steps in the right direction. It remains to be seen if they represent isolated exceptions.

I set Brecht's play in the Saudi Arabian desert to reflect the current reality of the oil business. The actors performed the scenes realistically. Songs in the script, with music composed for the occasion by Rusty McGee, interrupted the goings on. Addressed directly to the audience, they commented on the action and the characters' internal states. At the end, I had the cast line the edge of the stage, facing full front, and drive the lesson home.

One night, a young woman from Germany, who was visiting a friend in New Haven, happened to attend the play. She had seen a production in Nuremberg where the actors stood at lecterns and harangued the audience, and she preferred that version. In her estimation, it was more didactic and closer to the spirit of Brecht.

I didn't argue, although I knew from my own studies that Brecht was more flexible and varied in his theatrical pronouncement and practices. He may have used "alienation effects," like painting the faces of the king's assassins clown white in his production of Christopher Marlowe's *Edward II*. But he also spent an hour teaching the actors playing the murderers how to tie a noose properly. He wanted to make sure that they got the realistic stage business right. Having grown up in Germany for my first 12 years, I was also familiar with the Teutonic penchant for intellectualism divorced from reality and love for long-winded discussions. But I resisted quipping that, if German theater audiences aren't bored for at least half an hour watching a play, they don't think they're getting their money's worth; even though I knew that her preferred interpretation would have bombed in New Haven.

Regarding directing concepts, the thing to ask yourself is: Would you do the same staging of *Hamlet* in New York City as in Austin, Texas, or San Francisco, California?

If you say yes because you believe great art is universal, you might want to read the marvelous and entertaining article, "Shakespeare in the Bush," in which anthropologist Laura Bohannan recounts her effort to tell the story of *Hamlet* to the elders of the Tiv tribe in West Africa. As soon as she mentions that "the old chief" appeared as a ghost to Hamlet, the elders disagree with her, insisting that he was an omen, possibly an animated creature or a zombie sent by a witch. As Bohannan continues, they keep correcting her account. In the end, after a dying Hamlet manages to kill his uncle with his machete (!), the elders conclude that it was a good story, which she told with very few mistakes. They encourage her to share more tales from her country so they can instruct her in their true meaning!

In some cases, how to approach a play set in a particular location is straightforward. When I directed *Coyote Ugly*, Richard Mays, the costume designer, was delighted that the setting was Arizona. He'd grown up there and wanted to put everyone in Bermuda shorts because it was the favorite attire in the state during the hot summer months. I thought about it and said, "No. In New Haven and the Northeast, audiences think of people in Arizona as cowboys. They expect them to wear boots, jeans, cowboy shirts and bolo ties. If we put the actors in Bermuda shorts, they'll think we made a mistake."

But if it's not a matter of dress and you insist on the same approach regardless of venue, you're probably more interested in your own vision and concept than in connecting with your audience. Nothing wrong with that—that's how innovations happen and new ideas enter the world—but you better take the time to get it right and make it work. Remember the words of the great screenwriting teacher Robert McKee, "Having a good concept is like playing the kazoo on the steps of Carnegie Hall."

And don't be surprised when the cultural "philistines" turn their backs on you.

THE PLAY'S THE THING

I saw the original Broadway production of Bernard Pomerance's *The Elephant Man*—not the one starring Bradley Cooper, but the one with Philip Anglim playing Joseph Merrick, the severely misshapen Englishman who suffered from a genetic disorder called Proteus syndrome. There was a breath-taking moment when the character of Madge Kendall, touched by his sensitivity, reaches out and makes contact with his deformed hand. Carole Shelley, the actress playing Kendall, had made the decision impulsively in rehearsal, and the director, Jack Hofsiss, agreed to keep it, even though the gesture wasn't in the script.

It was deeply moving, but the playwright loathed it. He found the gesture too sentimental. He was probably correct, historically—no Victorian Englishwoman in her proper, right mind would have done so. But, ultimately, he had to admit that it had a powerful emotional impact. Perhaps he had forgotten his roots. Pomerance had grown up on Long Island, but he spent most of his playwriting career in England and had adopted the more hard-nosed, stiff-upper-lip, British attitude toward sentiment. Different cultures, different audience perceptions and reactions.

That doesn't mean directors should kowtow to their audiences and oversimplify or sentimentalize the material. Spectators are pretty savvy and can tell when you're condescending to them. But theater is a performance art whose magic occurs in the live encounter between actors and spectators. Both sides must be fully invested.

The relationship between directors and living playwrights can be contentious and strained. Dramatists, unhappy with bad or adventurous productions, often fantasize about making their plays actor- and director-proof. Samuel Beckett was furious when he heard that JoAnne Akalaitis staged *Endgame* not as he had written it but in a subway with African-American actors playing the parts of Hamm and Clove. Late in his career, Edward Albee always insisted on directing the world premieres of his plays before giving anyone else a shot so he could be sure to realize what he intended. The results were mixed.

I have come across only two plays that seem to be "idiot" proof. No matter what atrocities directors, designers and actors inflict on them, they have a compelling impact.

One is *A Midsummer Night's Dream*. I attended a dreadful production directed by James Lapine at the Delacorte Theater in Central Park in Manhattan. William Hurt, dressed like a Native American tribal chief, played Oberon as if he was on Valium laced with LSD. Marcell Rosenblatt, the actress cast as Puck, cavorted around the stage like an annoying, buzzing fly. But by the end, in part because of the hilarious Pyramus-Thisbe scene providing comic relief, the magic of the play remained undimmed.

The other indestructible drama is no longer well known in this country. Peter Weiss's *Marat/Sade* takes off from a quirky footnote of French history. The play is set in the Charenton lunatic asylum where the Marquis de Sade was tucked away when the French Revolution yielded to Napoleon's Empire. To pass the time, de Sade wrote and performed plays using the inmates as actors, and it became a lark for the newly minted aristocracy to attend his productions. The particular play being offered is about the assassination of Jean-Paul Marat, one of the leaders of the Reign of Terror, by Charlotte Corday. Since the actors are also inmates, they have to be kept in line by guards throughout the performance. There are rousing songs and moments of high theatricality—de Sade has Corday whip him with her long tresses—all in the service of a searing, yet entertaining meditation on the nature of human cruelty, rebellion and desire for freedom.

You can check out the film version of a remarkable theater production by Peter Brook and the Royal Shakespeare Company on *YouTube*, starring a young Glenda Jackson as the narcoleptic inmate who plays Corday and Patrick Magee as de Sade. I have seen two other stagings of *Marat/Sade*, both college productions, one mediocre, the other, workmanlike. Despite involving young, inexperienced actors and directors, they both transcended their limitations and packed a powerful punch.

Which brings me to the point that a good playwright always wins, regardless of what a director might think or want.

When I lived in New York, my former directing teacher, Tony Giordano, asked me to come to his production of Chekhov's *The Three Sisters*, performed by undergraduates in NYU's theater department. He warned me that none of the actors was good enough to embody any of the characters fully. However, he wanted to get my take on his interpretation—that the end of the play is a positive affirmation. According to Tony, the three sisters, Masha, Olga and Irina, despite failing in all their romantic and social aspirations, have found a new, hopeful purpose: They will bring learning and enlightenment to the Russian backwater village.

I shared my doubts. Chekhov is one the cruelest playwrights I know. In his human comedy, characters always end up defeated and have to figure out how to endure, knowing that tomorrow will creep "in this petty pace" for the remainder of their lives. It's melancholy at best, downright depressing at worst. Tony is one of the most positive people I have ever met, with high energy and fighting spirit, but I didn't think he'd manage to overcome a Russian playwright so adept at documenting emotional misery.

The production was excellent, well-paced and beautifully staged. Tony had lifted the cast up, both individually and as a company, and they performed at a level none of them imagined themselves capable of achieving. But at the end, predictably, they play took a nosedive, like a car plummeting off a cliff. Afterward, over drinks, Tony admitted defeat.

You can't keep a good playwright down, or lift him up, if he or she is determined to plunge into the abyss!

It's no different in film. The screenplay matters—more so than producers and directors want to admit or pay lip service to at the Academy Awards. They often start shooting too early, sometimes even before the writers have finished; but no director, however inventive, can fix a mediocre script. The current Hollywood love affair with special effects and blowing things up can't hide a shortage of good, character-driven stories.

At the same time, too many screenwriters direct their own works. My heart always sinks when I see "written and directed by ___" in the credits before the movie starts. I know that, in all likelihood, I'll be sitting through a turkey. All-too-often I'm right and walk out afterward thinking: Here was the opportunity to make an engrossing film. Too bad it didn't happen.

There are exceptions: Christopher Nolan's *Dunkirk*, David Hare's *Worricker* trilogy with Bill Nighy, a few French films by Truffaut and Goddard from the time when the notion of the cinema *auteur* who can do it all was born. But more often than not, a screenwriter who finally has the power to direct fails to realize that collaborating with a good filmmaker would improve the final product immensely.

The reason for these egotistic failures is that most writers have no idea what they have created and, as directors, only compound their mistakes. Without another perspective, they direct what they have put consciously into the script. But great dramatists and screenwriters can count on their unconscious to be fully engaged as well, contributing further layers and dimensions to their works. That's why they continue to speak to us, even centuries after they were created. A good director will mine both overt and covert material and shine a light on both.

The process of writer-director collaboration can lead to both amusing and frustrating moments in new play development.

My third year at the Drama School, I directed a workshop production of *Lives and Deaths of the Great Harry Houdini* by David Ives, who has since written well-received plays and adaptations, including *All in the Timing* and *Venus in Furs*. David had been fascinated with the Hungarian escape artist for a while and was doing large-scale rewrites, whole acts at a time. At first, he welcomed my suggestions, but when I objected to the direction he was taking, he got mad at me.

One of the character in the play was Houdini's manager-producer Sy Gesund. In German his name means "Be well" or "Be healthy," as in *Gesundheit!* David liked to play with words already, a hallmark of his witty style. Imagine my surprise when on the next go-around, Sy had a fatal accident in Act II, unrelated to anything required by the play. I knew right away what that was about and, without commenting, made peace with David regarding the way he wanted to develop the play. Sure enough, in the next draft, Sy was back fit as a fiddle until the finish. I don't know if David did it on purpose just to mess with me, or if his unconscious was furiously working overtime. We never discussed it. The play went well enough as a workshop production but remained unfinished.

Sometimes, a director will stage and reveal emotional aspects that the writer hasn't fully dealt with yet. Or an actor will make choices that are too close to the bone and the playwright becomes uncomfortable. I remember a student actor in another *Winterfest* production complaining about the rocky process. He'd been cast in a role especially close to the playwright's heart. On several occasions, when he thought rehearsal went well—the director was pleased—the next day the playwright had rewritten his part. Some of the more revealing lines ended up in the mouths of other characters. Some disappeared altogether.

Most experienced writers know better than to deny what comes to light, even if unexpected and painful. But as far as staging their own works, no matter how visually oriented they may be, above all, playwrights are wordsmiths. Many are (or were) good actors, which gives their dialogue extra resonance—Shakespeare, Moliere, Noel Coward, Harold Pinter, Sam Shepard, Lin-Manuel Miranda. If they are good directors as well, they usually do their best when tackling the works of fellow playwrights, not their own.

All artists work from their limitations. The good ones realize it and know to invite others to help them broaden their boundaries.

This is a good lesson for all of us: No one can do everything. Work from your strengths, get help to shore up your weaknesses and embrace collaborating—warts and all. You will be much more productive than if you try to tackle things on your own.

TAKING ADVICE

Everybody's a critic. Whether you're performing onstage or in a film, writing a play, painting, sculpting, cooking…everybody will want to put in their two cents worth. The problem is that it's hard to separate helpful advice from irrelevant input by people riding their favorite hobby horse.

I've seen playwrights show drafts too early and lose their play in the process. Heeding everyone's suggestions before they knew what it was about, they became discombobulated and mucked it up beyond repair.

Nothing is more frustrating to a stage director than to have friends, lovers or spouses of cast members attend a run-through of the play, only to see all the notes they gave afterward show up in rehearsal the next day. The changes usually run counter to what the production demands, and getting the performances back on track takes time and considerable diplomacy.

Close to opening, many actors get anxious and look for validation wherever they can find it. I saw a preview of an excellent production of Ibsen's *The Master Builder* in New York. The lead was played by an actor I had worked with two years earlier. When I went backstage to say hello, he asked me, "Any notes?" I said, "You're doing fine and your director is doing great work with you. Trust him."

I know many theater people who would not have resisted the urge to comment in more detail.

That is not to say you don't need outside help from time to time. I was at assisting Lloyd Richards on *Uncle Vanya* when James Earl Jones came to see him. They were old friends and had worked together the year before on Ibsen's *Hedda Gabler* at the Yale Rep. Jones was in rehearsals for a Broadway production of *Othello* in which he played the Moor opposite Christopher Plummer's Iago, and he was in despair. Lloyd told me that Jones said, "I've done this play seven times, but I'm lost with the role."

I don't know what advice Lloyd gave him. I went to see the production, directed by Peter Coe who had overseen the dreadful *Hamlet* in Stratford a few years back, and it was not a pretty experience either. Coe was a well-established director who'd had great success with the movie version of the musical *Oliver*, but he seemed at a loss with Shakespeare performed by American actors. Still, everyone onstage, except Dianne Wiest who played Desdemona as a petulant child, acquitted themselves well. Whenever Jones wasn't sure of what he was saying or doing, he'd lower his voice an octave. I could feel it caress the back of my neck and forgave him everything.

Plummer spoke the verse very well but gave a mannered, formalistic performance. In one soliloquy, when he uttered, "I shall enmesh them all," he turned the "sh" at the end of "enmesh" into an elongated, hissing shudder to demonstrate just how evil Iago was and to wow the audience. It was as calculated a star turn as it was ludicrous, but some of the spectators gasped—great acting as far as they were concerned. The critics were wowed, too.

I rode the train back to New Haven with Bern Sundstedt, who had graduated from the drama school at the end of my first year and still lived in town with his girlfriend. Bern played a number of minor characters in the production and told me that Plummer had it in his contract that no one onstage was allowed to move during his soliloquies—big ego on parade!

Bern also mentioned that Dianne Wiest had been suffering from a cold for several performances and found it difficult to lie still on Desdemona's deathbed. Fortunately, when Iago drew his sword and tried to castrate Othello—another gratuitous Plummer innovation—the audience gasped again, this time in horror, allowing her to cough into her pillows unnoticed.

"Weapons" with which to divert and trick spectators should be in the arsenal of every director.

But getting back to seeking help when you're feeling at sea or have hit a creative wall, here are two stories about playwrights listening to advice:

During tryouts for Neil Simon's comedy *The Odd Couple*, the famous Boston theater critic Elliot Norton gave the play a positive review but mentioned that the third act was lacking something. When he interviewed Simon on his radio show, he commented, "You know who I missed in the third act was the Pigeon Sisters." They had appeared earlier in the play.

Simon later said that it was like a light bulb going on in his head and he rewrote the play accordingly. He generously credited Norton, telling the *Boston Globe*, "Elliot had such a keen eye. I don't know if he saved the play or not, but he made it a bigger success."

The other story came from Frank Torok, my first-year directing teacher, who had been production stage manager in 1971 when Terence McNally's *Where has Tommy Flowers Gone?* had its premiere at the Yale Rep. The play tells the story of a happy-go-lucky, social misfit from the 1960s who has a hard time adjusting as he gets older and crosses the threshold from youthful rebellion to adulthood (Abbie Hoffman, a radical Yippie from that era, famously said, "Never trust anyone over 30.")

During rehearsals, one of the actors had difficulties with a monologue. He couldn't get a certain section and insisted that the problem was in the writing. After much arguing back and forth, McNally revised the speech and everybody was happy with the results.

When the play moved to New York, the actor didn't stay with the show because of a prior commitment. For the auditions to replace him, the production team used the original monologue, and another actor nailed it without any difficulties. The lesson for McNally was: He would rewrite any line or speech that gave an actor difficulty for a particular production, but until at least three actors stumbled at the same spot, he wouldn't change it for the printed version.

So, take what people tell you about your work with a big shaker of salt; or, if you're on a salt-free diet, with a big dose of vinegar. When in doubt, keep your own counsel. Don't assume they, whoever they are, know what they're talking about, no matter what their reputation, pedigree or professional experience. At best, people can tell you what's not working for them. They may be putting their fingers on a spot that needs attention. But it's up to you to fix it. Norton gave Neil Simon a great suggestion, but it was Simon who rewrote the third act.

It gets tricky when you find yourself in really serious trouble. At that point, it's essential to seek help and advice elsewhere, preferably from people you can trust to know their stuff and have your best interest at heart.

GET A BOARD OF DIRECTORS

We all could use a personal board of directors who support us when we try something new and help out when we get into trouble. But most people want to deal with problems alone, like small children who try to assert their independence and insist to Mommy, "I can do it myself!"

The idea of the lone cowboy, so enshrined in American culture, is actually a made-up notion that has nothing to do with the real Wild West. We owe that fantasy to Hollywood. As David Milch, the creator of the marvelous HBO series *Deadwood*, has pointed out: Cattle wranglers coming off the trail were a gregarious, foul-mouthed bunch who loved to swear, whoop it up, and tell stories and tall tales.

The few determined loners—Jeremiah Johnson and other early scouts and explorers—were misfits and, in some cases, psychotics or sociopaths. American civilization west of the Mississippi was built on cooperation and exploitation (primarily of Native Americans), not by lone gunslingers.

But when oaters became a favorite movie staple, the production code of the 1930s and 40s prohibited the use of foul language. This notion may seem absurd to people used to current cable TV fare. But remember, it was not too long ago, during Watergate, that many Americans were stunned when the Nixon tapes were released—all those "expletive deleted" gaps in the transcript. They were shocked not only because it turned out that Nixon was a crook, but because the President of the United States was as crude and foul-mouthed as a lowlife Mafioso.

Give good writers limitations, and they will rise to the occasion. Deprived of the juicy, colorful language of actual cowboys, Hollywood screenwriters invented the strong, silent type, the taciturn hero whose quietness speaks volumes, with a welter of emotion churning beneath the laconic exterior. Unfortunately, many people continue to buy into the myth and think that they have to do everything on their own. For creative people, this foolishness finds support in other Hollywood fantasies about lone, tortured geniuses like Michelangelo (*The Agony and the Ecstasy*), Van Gogh (*Lust for Life*), and more recently, Jackson Pollock (*Pollock*), Frida Kahlo (*Frida*) and William Turner (*Mr. Turner*).

Considering that film and theater are labor-intensive art forms, which rely on the collaboration of many talented people, you'd think that screenplays would reflect that experience. But perhaps because writing can be a lonely profession, writers overidentify with the Lone Cowboy archetype and are reluctant to let it go, even though he has long outlived his purpose and can cuss freely now like the rest of us.

In the theater, most successful actors and directors rely on friends and colleagues they trust to be a sounding board or second pair of eyes at some stage in their creative process. Directors will invite other directors to a run-through prior to technical rehearsals, previews and opening to tell them what they think works and what doesn't.

Ideally, actors trust their director to guide them to a good performance. However, in movies that is no longer the case. In the old days, many directors first cut their teeth in the theater and had considerable experience working with actors. Now, most of them graduate from film schools having watched a lot of movies, but with little or no understanding of the acting process.

I got my first job staging an opera when Nelson Sheeley asked me if I wanted to take over a production he'd been slated to direct at Bel Canto Opera in New York. He was artistic director of a summer stock theater in Pennsylvania and had fallen behind in his planning for the season. The piece was *The Poacher*, a comic opera by Albert Lortzing, a mid-19th-century German composer. Lortzing is not well-known in this country, but in German opera houses, rarely a season goes by without one of his works on the schedule.

Of course, I said Yes!, but I knew I was in over my head. So, I called up two of my former directing teachers. David Hammond, who had staged a number of operas in California, gave me excellent advice: Let the singers take care of the words and story as written in the libretto and move them around the stage according to the score. A good composer will put all kinds of things into the music—thought pauses and mincing steps, the instant when Tosca plunges a dagger into Scarpia's chest, and the exact moment when Siegfried pulls the sword from the trunk of an oak tree in Wagner's *The Valkyrie*.

My other teacher, Tony Giordano, congratulated me and said, "You need help. You can't do this on your own." He found me an assistant. Mark Ramont was starting out in New York as a young director, too, and wanted to learn about opera. He proved invaluable. I couldn't have done it without him looking over my shoulder.

One scene in the first act called for the arrival of a large hunting party, led by the hero, a melancholy, young baron. Being a small opera company, all we could muster for the male chorus were four huntsmen, but the French horn and trumpet fanfares suggested a grand entrance. So, I choreographed an elaborate parade sending the quartet of singing hunters all over the stage before they finally settled in front of the baron to listen to his aria. (In opera, you try to place people downstage of the singers and looking at them whenever possible, so they have a reason to aim their solos toward the audience.)

I turned to Mark and asked, "What do you think?" He shook his head judiciously and said, "I don't think it works."

His expression was more to the point. It told me I had concocted a disaster, and he was right. Fortunately, I had another idea and re-staged the hunters trying to cheer up their downhearted, feudal lord. The more intimate scene told a different visual story that worked surprisingly well—entrance saved, embarrassment avoided!

Here is a cautionary tale of what happened to someone who went solo without a safety net.

Steve Hendrickson who graduated two years ahead of me from the drama school was the first actor in his class to get a plum of a job in television after he auditioned for *Archie's Bunker's Place*. The show was a spin-off of Norman Lear's *All in the Family* and also starred Carroll O'Connor, who had originated the role of Archie Bunker, the lovable, blue-collar bigot. Steve can be a very funny guy, and he had the director, producers and casting agent falling out of their chairs with laughter. Although they were looking for a chubby Italian as a sidekick for Archie, they hired him.

Television City Studios flew Steve to California and had him picked up at the airport in a limo. Everything was done first-class. The driver welcomed him to LA and kept up a friendly patter during the ride. There were costume fittings and, before long, Steve had a wardrobe of fancy suits and other fashionable outfits.

Although he kept asking for a script, he didn't get one until Sunday night before the first rehearsal. When he read it, he was appalled. Steve knew funny and this script wasn't. But he figured that maybe the producers and writers knew what they were doing, and things would turn out better in the morning.

When he arrived on the set, the director took him aside and said, "Steve, I have to tell you, that was the funniest audition I have ever seen in my life. I nearly peed in my pants, but…it's not what we want."

Steve was stunned. Recovering quickly, he ventured, "I can be flexible. What are you looking for?"

The answer: "We don't know…but we'll know when we see it."

After this auspicious beginning, rehearsals went on all week. Every evening the writers huddled and came back with a new script the next day. Carroll O'Connor was standoffish. Steve's suggestions for improving some of the lines for his side-kick character fell on deaf ears.

On Friday before the taping, there was a dress rehearsal for the producers. Ten suits from CBS, Tandem Productions and Television City Studios strutted onto the sound stage and took front row seats to render judgment and approval. The run-through commenced. Whenever Carroll O'Connor said something, the executives fell over themselves with laughter. Whenever Steve had a line, they responded with deathly silence.

The same thing happened the next episode. That Friday, Steve came upon the associate producer going through his clothes rack, picking out a suit for himself.

After the taping, when Steve left his dressing room, the sound stage was empty, as if the rats had deserted a sinking ship. He walked back to the studio offices, also empty, except for the receptionist who told him his car to the airport was waiting. The same driver, so friendly and chatty upon his arrival, did not say a word. Steve felt as if all of LA knew of his status as a pariah. No one at the studio ever told him he was fired. The bad news was delivered to his agent, and Steve found out from him.

The producers hired someone to play the fat Italian side-kick to Carroll O'Connor they had wanted all along.

I believe that there are several lessons in this horror story. The most important: Get support when you're in trouble! Steve was too young and inexperienced in the business to realize that he needed help, desperately! He should have called up friends and former teachers for advice. That may not have saved his job, but it would have made the experience less traumatic than going through it alone. Instead, he learned cold turkey just how brutal the entertainment business can be—full of people whose social skills would make a Neanderthal blush.

By the way, that was not the end of the story. Sometime later, Steve ran into one of his co-stars from the TV show in New York. According to her, by the end of the first season, his character who appeared in only two episodes received a surprising amount of positive fan mail.

I worked with Steve a few years later in the production of Ibsen's *A Doll House* at Playmaker's Rep in North Carolina. He played Dr. Rank, the physician who lives upstairs from Nora and Torvald Helmer. By then, Steve had left his Hollywood experience far behind and was enjoying a successful career in regional theaters. He was easy to work with and brought a lot of good ideas to rehearsals. His sensitive portrayal of the dying doctor who is secretly in love with Nora was understated and very moving.

There is another important lesson to draw from Steve's sorry Hollywood tale. If you ever hear someone in the entertainment industry say, "We don't know…but we'll know when we see it…"—Run! As far away as possible, as fast as you can. That goes for other walks of life as well.

Too many people in positions of authority have no clue what they're doing but act like they're the big enchilada. If you're working for an ignorant, narcissistic egomaniac, you are bound to get into trouble. You may luck out and give him exactly what he's looking for the first time around. So much the worse. Now you're on a tall pedestal and, when you don't deliver the next time, you'll crash down that much harder.

UNINTENDED CONSEQUENCES

People often make references to the "Law of Unintended Consequences" when something unforeseen happens. It's really more of a concept than an ironclad law, but everyone understands that actions often produce unexpected results. The idea holds true in all aspects of life and has theatrical manifestations from the silly to the sublime. Usually, the outcome runs counter to the original intent, but not always. Sometimes, it's just an interesting sideshow that no one foresaw.

Nelson Sheeley told me about a comedy at a summer theater in Buck's County, Pennsylvania, in which the director decided it would be fun to have one of the characters come onstage with two piglets under his arms. The actor, a sturdy lad, was game. Since they were in farm country, it wasn't hard to get hold of two suitable candidates. The play opened and the two young pigs were a great hit with the audiences. What no one had anticipated was that they defecated profusely wherever and whenever they felt like it, often at the most inopportune moments. Nor had anyone considered how fast they would grow. By the middle of the run, the two cute little oinkers had turned into hefty sows who were increasingly harder to lift and control. They were stubborn, too. They refused to take a bow.

Sometimes the results run counter to the predictable negative outcome, much to the frustration of the people who initiated the action.

Early in his career as artistic director of Florida Studio Theatre in Sarasota, Richard Hopkins put on *La Ronde* by the Austrian playwright, Arthur Schnitzler. A comedy of manners satirizing the sexual mores of 19th-century Vienna, the title is often rendered into English as *The Merry-Go-Round*. Written in 1897, the play has ten interlocking, two-character scenes, in which members from all levels of Viennese society pair up and go to bed with each other. One of the two paramours appears in the next scene, creating a chain of couplings that finishes with a count meeting the whore, who started the play seducing a soldier—hence the title suggesting a circular journey.

There is no foul language in the play, and the sexual trysts are handled discretely and theatrically by the characters going offstage and the lights dimming to black for a moment. But the implied eroticism and open acknowledgment of carnal affairs shocked the audiences at the premieres in Berlin in 1920 and a year later, in Vienna. Critics and the public vilified the play and attacked Schnitzler with anti-Semitic slurs, calling him a Jewish pornographer.

Fast forward 60 years and, in the words of the French journalist and critic Alphonse Karr, "Plus ça change, plus c'est la même chose"—or, "Same-old, same-old."

During a matinee performance of the play in Sarasota in the early 1980s, some members of the audience were so offended that they started to complain out loud. The heckling swelled into a chant of "Stop this filth, stop this filth, stop this filth." At some point, the two actors onstage halted the scene and refused to continue until the hecklers left the theater.

The intensity of the response to the play caught everyone at FST by surprise. The unintended consequence was that, once word got out about the incident, including news coverage in the *Sarasota Herald Tribune*, the show was sold out for the rest of the run.

A common situation that occurs onstage with unexpected results is an actor going off-script. My high school drama teacher,

Paul Yager, was a post-middle-age character actor with a whiskey-stained voice who still performed in professional theaters around the Chicago area. He was very good, but his memory had seen better days. During long monologues, he'd get lost and start to meander, keeping the other actors onstage in suspense. Would he find his way to the next cue line? Surprisingly, he always did.

But Paul also dropped lines from time to time. I attended a performance when he did just that. I knew the play and realized what had happened, but no one else in the audience caught on that he was the culprit because he stood still onstage while all the other actors around him scrambled, ad-libbing like crazy to get back on track.

In film, such mishaps are immortalized in outtakes and blooper reels, which sometimes become part of the credits or appear as extras on the DVD release. In the theater, the unintended consequence is that the perpetrator comes off smelling like a rose and everyone else looks like a frenetic skunk.

In my own experience, there have been several occasions when the law of unintended consequences held sway.

Perhaps the most significant instance occurred during my time at the Yale School of Drama as a result of a production I mounted in the spring of my first year at the student-run cabaret. The play was *Shakespeare the Sadist* by Wolfgang Bauer. Written in 1971, the dark, satirical comedy examines the roles women get to play in movies (the German title, *Film und Frau—Film and Woman*—is more to the point).

In short, jump cut scene fragments, skipping in time, we see three, 20-something guys and a young woman hang out in a run-down city apartment. As they talk about movies to relieve their boredom, she mocks and belittles them at every turn. At some point, the men decide to go and see a porn flick. The one they pick happens to have the same title as the play, *Shakespeare the Sadist*.

The audience then gets to "see" the film onstage, set in the same apartment. The woman (Sonia), now dressed in a negligee, is waiting for Shakespeare (Bill), played by one of the men. When he arrives, he carries two suitcases. One contains his sonnets and plays; the other, whips, handcuffs and chains. After reading her some of his poems—in pidgin Swedish with projected subtitles—they engage in an over-the-top sequence of acrobatic sex, which I staged with strobe lights and throbbing musical underscoring. At the climax, Shakespeare saws off Sonia's head, holds it up and, like the gravedigger in *Hamlet* addressing a skull, says, "Alas, poor Yorick."

The regular play resumes as the three men return from their outing, dissecting the sleazy movie they've just seen like serious film buffs. In the final scene, they play poker, wearing cowboy hats. Suddenly, Sonia bursts into the room a la Annie Oakley, dressed in fringed leather chaps and wearing a big Stetson. Brandishing a revolver, she takes revenge and shoots the three misogynists dead.

The play is outlandish and wildly funny yet has a serious message. Bauer was trying to make the point that, for actresses in the 1970s and early 1980s, film roles were limited to bitch goddess, femme fatale, sex symbol, victim, and cowgirl. Those options are still with us. The cowgirl, for example, has morphed into female action characters—Maggie Q, Scarlett Johansson, Jennifer Lawrence, Charlize Theron, and Gal Gadot kicking ass in movies and television shows like *Designated Survivor*, *The Avengers*, *The Hunger Games*, *Mad Max: Fury Road*, *Atomic Blonde*, and *Wonder Woman*.

The recent revelations about Bill Cosby, Harvey Weinstein and other male sexual predators exposed an on-going sexist culture in Hollywood. While many women are fighting back against these abusers, others are also working to broaden the range of female roles. The successes of actresses turned writers and producers, like Lena Dunham, Greta Gerwig and Reese Witherspoon, and shows like

Girls, *Lady Bird*, *Big Little Lies* and *Hidden Figures*, are a welcome and long overdue development.

But in the long run, addressing the systemic nature of female exploitation in the entertainment industry will prove more difficult than unmasking the most obvious perpetrators. Like it or not, women continue to occupy the uneasy roles of being sexualized and marketed for their physical attributes, both by the film and fashion industry. Just consider the collective cleavage shown at any recent award show—Oscars, Emmys, Tonys. Although there is considerably more male skin on view in films since Paul Newman took off his shirt in *Cat on a Hot Tin Roof* and *Cool Hand Luke*, none of the male presenters or winners look like sex symbols in their elegant evening wear. Not a single one displays his pecs, rippling abs or muscular backs.

I'm not suggesting we return to Victorian or Puritan times and cover everyone up. Too many Arab extremists insist their women do so, and look at the oppression that comes with that. But Western societies have entrenched views of women, too, and the roles they're supposed to play don't make for easy transitions to true liberation and equality. The cultural messaging of traditional prejudice is pervasive and often unconscious.

For a minor example, take *Wheel of Fortune* (besides Vanna White's secondary role as letter-turning hostess). In the final round, if the contestant is a woman, Pat Sajak always takes her by the hand and leads her to a designated line on the studio floor. If its a man, he merely points to it. Surely the show's producers don't think that women can't get there on their own.

I recently saw a poster on display at the St. Petersburg Museum of Art (the one in Florida, not in Russia) by Guerilla Girls, a group of feminist activist artists. It posed the provocative question, "Do women have to be naked to get into the Met Museum?" and continued, "Less than 5% of the artists in the Modern Art sections are women, but 85% of the nudes are female."

According to the Institute for Women's Policy Research, in 2017, full-time, year-round female workers earned only 80.5 cents for every dollar made by men. The gap is even wider for Black and Hispanic women. Megan Rapino and her teammates demanding the same pay as professional male players before and after they won the 2019 World Soccer Cup drew attention to just one instance of the material inequalities women face.

The discussions and actions must reach far beyond exposing, shaming and punishing powerful men for their abuses if we are to institute real changes.

As for *Shakespeare the Sadist*, we tried hard to make sure audiences understood the play as satire. Rick Butler, my set designer, created an animated short for the opening to establish a comedic tone: Shakespeare's face appeared inside the MGM logo, opening and closing his mouth like the famous lion, to the sounds of the Twentieth Century Fox intro music. I also used well-known music themes from films of the era during the blackouts between scenes—*The Godfather*, *Rocky*, *The Magnificent Seven*, to name a few—to reinforce the sense of watching a movie. For the final "clip," over-sized poker cards suggested a heightened, hyperbolic Western fantasy.

Casting the three male actors was easy. Pat Skipper, Vyto Ruginis and Bern Sundstedt were always game for pushing the envelope and readily agreed. Finding someone to play the female role proved to be a challenge, however. The only actress willing was an intrepid British dramaturg student, Philippa Keil, and she was great. Frances McDormand helped with makeup, putting a semi baldpate on Vyto to make him look like a derelict.

Most spectators got the humor and had a good time. My undergraduate German professor, Peter Demetz, came and laughed himself silly. The response of my fellow drama school students was mixed, however. After the Friday night opening—we had another show on Saturday—a number of male acting students came backstage to offer their congratulations, but only one female actor showed up: Kate Burton. She was complimentary and thought the production was funny (as a Brit, she was perhaps more comfortable with the tradition of outrageous satire). When none of her American counterparts made an appearance, I figured that the play had struck a nerve and pissed them off. Both my hunches were confirmed the following year when an actress liked how I was working with her in rehearsals for a new play workshop production and decided to clear the air. She told me that she and her peers had been furious with me after seeing the play and thought I was a sexist pig.

None of the faculty that mattered saw the play—the top brass of the drama school had been away at a theater conference—but word got around, of course. Although I was never called on the carpet for the production, I'm pretty sure I developed a reputation as something of a weirdo with bizarre tastes.

The consequence, unintended on my part, was that my second-year directing teacher heard about it, too, and recommended I do that marvelous play of sublime grotesquery, *The Bewitched*, for my thesis project. When I proposed it, the faculty gave me the green light without objections.

Sometimes, the universe swipes at you; sometimes, it whacks you; and sometimes, it gives you a nod.

ALL IN THE FAMILY

Western drama is a unique art form that deals primarily with human conflict in action. There are exceptions— avant-garde creations that stretch the boundaries both in form and content. I saw an experimental play by JoAnne Akalaitis at the Wooster Group in New York, which consisted of a 20-minute, voiceover monologue while a large amber crystal rotated on a pedestal onstage, throwing off scintillating light. It might have worked as performance art in a museum, but as a theater offering, it was pretentious and boring. For the most part, plays and films do better when telling stories about human beings struggling with one another to get something they want.

That being the case, it is no wonder that so many plays and movies deal with unhappy families. From the *Oresteia* to *Hamlet* and *King Lear* to Ibsen's *A Doll House*, all of Chekhov's plays, Francis Ford Coppola's *Godfather* movies, and TV shows like *Dallas* and *Empire*, the personal battles take place on domestic grounds. Many TV comedy shows, from the early days of *Leave it to Beaver* and *My Three Sons* to *Modern Family*, humorously tackle family conflicts.

I like to tell people that I come from a wonderfully dysfunctional family, which gave me all the experiences and preparation I needed for a career in the arts. I say it ironically and most people chuckle; but, of course, there is a serious side to it: Growing up after my parents divorced didn't feel like a fun ride in an amusement park.

Unfortunately, most of us don't live long enough to get over our upbringing and heal all the wounds. Every generation repeats the mistakes of its predecessors or reacts against them by going to opposite extremes. Which is probably why so many classic plays continue to speak to us many centuries a later.

While that may be good for drama, it doesn't offer much optimism for the prospects of the human race. It's also why just about every American sci-fi author worth his or her salt—Isaac Asimov, L. Ron Hubbard, Octavia Butler—believed that humanity's future is in the stars. The idea of getting off this planet and leaving our problems behind relates to America's history of Westward Expansion and pioneer mentality. But that's another story.

Many plays and movies require actors and directors to call on their own family experiences and memories. The more specific they can get, the better, because when it comes to creating believable households, it's all in the details. Paradoxically, when people generalize about familial relations, audiences remain unconvinced. But put a flesh and blood Italian, Polish, Irish or African-American family with all its ethnic and cultural quirks in front of them, and they'll say, "That's just like *my* family."

In a 2017 *New York Times* article, an interviewer asked the actor Laurence Fishburne why more than 75% of the viewers of *black-ish*, a television comedy about a middle-class, African-American family, were white. He said, "We're trying to reach everybody that we can with the specificity of our culture and our experiences.... And if the numbers are any indication of how we're doing, the reality is that our experience is universal."

When it comes to exploring the emotional aspects of a character, a good trawling ground is high school. In certain ways, we're all teenagers at heart and continue to act like them. In the face of emotional challenges and intimate relationships, we often revert to earlier times, even when life demands a more mature approach. (Although adolescence is a fairly recent phenomenon. The idea of a 10-year stage between childhood and young adulthood dates back only to the first third of the 20th century.)

To understand the characters in a play, I recommend looking at them as teenagers in action. Imagine who they would have been in their high school years. It works well for all the couples in Shakespeare's *A Midsummer Night's Dream*, not just the young lovers lost in the woods, but also Theseus and Hippolyta and the feuding gods, Titania and Oberon. Think of Hamlet as an overgrown teenager, and a lot of his behavior and outbursts in the early acts make perfect sense.

When I directed *The Provok'd Wife* at Emory University in Atlanta, I stayed in a Bed and Breakfast within walking distance of the campus. Although I was 35 by then, I conceived the play as a comedy of manners about men and women still rooted in their teenage years, who long for love but feel anxious about commitment and marriage. I added a prologue to the play in which the major characters performed an "approach-avoidance" dance around a pair of mannequins dressed in wedding gown and tuxedo to a harpsichord rendition of the Rolling Stones' "I Can't Get No Satisfaction."

The play has a lot of sexual escapades and high jinx, and I related the behavior of all the characters, even the middle-aged ones, to the way I remembered high school: a minefield of emotions, fantasies, awkward self-consciousness, raging hormones, and over-the-top, expressive behavior. I encouraged lots of physicality—teenagers bump up to one another to show interest when words fail them. In the tavern scene that spilled out into the street, I had the old husband-rake drunkenly negotiate a hopscotch pattern chalked on the sidewalk.

The actors responded with ideas of their own. Brenda Bynum, playing the vain, middle-aged belle who has seen better days but imagines that everyone is slain by her beauty, added an inspired stutter whenever she uttered the words "my f-f-f-faults."

At the preview and on opening night, to my amazement, the spectators divided along gender lines. The men all laughed at certain jokes and funny situations, and the women found other comic moments and lines hilarious. I have never before or since experienced such a clear-cut, divided audience response.

The play, like all classical comedies, ends with the marriage of the young lovers. I conceived the epilogue as a goofy fertility dance, again accompanied by harpsichord, to the tune of the Stones' "You Can't Always Get What You Want," whose final line of the refrain put a cap on the show. As it segued into the curtain call, the divided audiences came together too, and, delighted with the outcome, applauded wildly.

For me, directing *The Provok'd Wife* had an additional bonus—an unintended consequence. The afternoon before the first preview, I went to my lodgings to take a nap and get ready for the evening. As I was lying in bed, I suddenly had the sensation of the ceiling opening up, and memories of all the good things I experienced in high school pouring down on me like a warm spring shower. Until then, I had always thought of my teenage years as an unhappy time, filled with loneliness, alienation and existential angst. This surprising, almost tactile experience was like a blessing—a big part of me that I had denied far too long suddenly unlocked and became available to me again. I felt an almost electric charge surge through my body, resetting muscle memories: a simultaneous letting go and integration.

Which brings me to the role of the unconscious in art.

GIVE THE SHADOW ITS DUE

Many people have experienced throwing out their back. It seems to happen in an instant—a shooting pain stabs you, often in some unreachable spot, indicating that a strained muscle or tendon has popped. Chiropractors, massage therapists, physical therapists and anti-inflammatory drugs can provide some relief, but it usually takes several days to get rid of the pain and tension.

The German word for this phenomenon is *Hexenschuss*—witches' shot—a more primal and poetic term. The compound word betrays its origin in medieval times when people believed that wicked fairies, hobgoblins and evil spirits surrounded them, and that witches had special powers to inflict harm directly and from a distance.

We tend to pooh-pooh such notions as childish superstitions, like the beliefs that it is bad luck to cross the path of a black cat, walk under a ladder, break a mirror, or spill salt during a meal. There are countermeasures for such transgressions—quickly tossing a pinch of salt over one's shoulder, carrying a rabbit's foot and saying "God Bless You" after someone sneezes.

Actors can be a superstitious lot, and the theater is rife with irrational beliefs. The tradition of leaving on a single light bulb upstage center when the theater is empty—the ghost light—is meant to ward off mischievous spirits. Having a bad dress rehearsal is considered good luck, guaranteeing a great opening night per-formance. That may be wishful thinking, but it does boost morale.

Some props supposedly create bad vibes onstage in their real incarnations—money, jewelry, flowers and Bibles. Peacock feathers are a no-no, too, because their "eyes" represent the Evil Eye, and they have been blamed for all kinds of disasters, including sets collapsing and theaters catching on fire.

There are other taboos, but by far the most terrible sin is to utter the name of Shakespeare's play *Macbeth* inside a theater rather than referring to it obliquely as "The Scottish Play." Culprits must ward off the curse by going outside and performing a cleansing ritual—turning around three times, spitting and knocking to be let back inside—or some variation thereof. Anecdotes about actors who did not heed the warning suffering fractured legs and ankles, getting stabbed accidentally onstage, slipping and even dying during a performance are part of theatrical lore going as far back as the 17th century.

I know of only one other play with such a cursed pedigree—*The Devils* by John Whiting, which chronicles demonic mass possession at a nunnery in a small French town in 1634. Based on Aldous Huxley's historical novel, *The Devils of Loudun*, it was later made into a controversial film by Ken Russell with Vanessa Redgrave as the abbess and Oliver Reed as the libertine priest accused of causing mass hysteria and satanic possession of her flock. The play teems with perverse sexual fantasies, exorcism, torture and burning at the stake and packs tremendous power in performance. And there are stories, of course, of accidents occurring during the mounting of the premiere in 1961 and a subsequent production.

I don't hold with superstitions and magical explanations for mysterious mishaps, but I do believe in the power of the unconscious.

I've mentioned Anne Baxter twisting her ankle prior to the opening of an awful production of *Hamlet*. Considering that actors wish each other good luck by saying "Break a leg," really hurting part of a limb to guard yourself against bad reviews and audience disapproval has an inspired kind of psychic symmetry.

When it comes to plays plagued by trouble, my take is not that they are cursed, but that their subject matter reaches deep into the darker recesses of our psyche. To the degree that we carry unresolved, repressed issues, we are vulnerable to internal forces rearing their ugly heads. After all, *Macbeth* and *The Devils* deal with witchcraft, evil spells, sexual frustration and satanic rituals. When "The Scottish Play" was written, most people believed in all kinds of malicious spirits. And judging by the popularity of horror movies, not just serial killers in scary masks, but films about ghosts and other supernatural occurrences, modern audiences continue to be fascinated and gleefully frightened by the possibility that such phenomena exist.

Most Americans are uncomfortable with the notion of the unconscious. They find it alarming and, like our emotions, impossible to control. Many refuse to believe it exists. But Sigmund Freud acknowledged its force and mapped some of its aspects in his seminal book *The Interpretation of Dreams*. The Swiss psychoanalyst, Carl Gustav Jung, extended it with concepts like archetypes, synchronicity and the Shadow.

Why is this important? Anything that digs deep into our deep-rooted fears and fantasies can haunt us, trip us up and trigger unexpected mayhem. Denied, it can rear up in destructive ways. So, if you're going to take on a dark play, you better be ready for it emotionally. As a director and surrogate father or mother of the acting company, you will be the keeper of a lot of people's anxiety. To the degree you can be free and easy about it and allay their fears, the production is more likely to come off without a hitch.

When I chose to direct *The Bewitched*, I knew that there were demonic aspects of the play that could become pitfalls for me. Although it is a wildly funny farce, it does deal with bewitchment, exorcism, the

Spanish Inquisition, impotence, evil mothers and other monstrosities—none of them pleasant, even if used for comic effect. I didn't want to tango too deeply with any of them. I certainly didn't want to get stuck with them. The production would end up grim and depressing rather than the feast of manic hilarity it should be. As a director, I knew I had to invite the Shadow into my consciousness.

So, as part of my preparation, I spent time meditating on the painful aspects and moments in the play, letting myself experience them from my perspective and from each character's point of view. Then, I created an artistic collage of darkness. It included drawings and paintings by Goya, Dali, El Greco, Francis Bacon, and Picasso—grotesque images in which pain distorts the human body beyond endurance. I hung it in my apartment, giving the murky underbelly of the play a place so that it would not invade my life during rehearsals and performances. And it worked! No mishaps or accidents occurred in the course of the production.

This notion of embracing the darker, unpleasant impulses of human existence goes back to the ancient Greeks. At the end of Aeschylus' *Oresteia*, which deals with the assassination of a king, matricide, and the clamor for revenge of these atrocities, the goddess Athena proposes a compromise to staunch further bloodletting. She offers a new role to the Furies who insist on savage payback. They will have a different name—Eumenides (the "gracious ones")—and have a sacred place of honor under her altar where they will act as the guardians of the administration of laws and justice. The Furies accept, and social order is restored; but they are only partially appeased and tamed, ready to exact their demands for bloody retribution at a moment's notice if things go awry.

The ancient Greeks understood that you must give the darkness its due. American society is still catching up to their discoveries. Although psychotherapists and psychiatrists have gotten better play in film and television in recent years, starting with Judd Hirsch in *Ordinary People* and Lorraine Bracco as Tony Soprano's shrink, most people still look down on people who seek professional help in real life.

Any artist worth his or her salt, not only acknowledges the existence of the unconscious but actively courts it and makes it part of the working process. Those who do so successfully experience the other side of the coin, too, where it acts as a creative force and allows intuition, dreams and unexpected ideas to flourish. The more attuned you are to them, the richer your work will be.

Again, it helps to be emotionally stable and of robust mental health, because there is a fine line between inspired creativity and madness; and some who step across it have a hard time coming back to normalcy and sanity. In the *Star Wars* saga, Anakin Skywalker yields to the seduction of the dark side of the Force and becomes permanently trapped by it as Darth Vader. As the German philosopher Friedrich Nietzsche famously wrote, "Beware that, when fighting monsters, you yourself do not become a monster…for when you gaze long into the abyss, the abyss gazes also into you."

I suspect that the current political anger and ugliness in American society is in part an expression of the Shadow denied. Our leaders have not addressed the fears and anxieties of people who don't know how to cope with our modern global economy and changing world. Unacknowledged, they have bubbled out into the open, encouraged by power mongers and purveyors of fear. Having unleashed the furies, we can only hope leaders will emerge who can unite us and help us return to a society of civility, laws and justice. We have had such leaders in times of crises in the past—the Founders and Framers of our country and the Constitution, Abraham Lincoln during the Civil War, Franklin Roosevelt in the Great Depression. But as a nation, we haven't adequately dealt with the horrors of our past, including slavery and the genocide of Native Americans. Nor have we resolved the pain and anxiety engendered by mass murder sprees at Sandy Hook, in Orlando and Parkland, and as of this writing, in Dayton and El Paso; or taken decisive legislative action. Instead, we continue to demonize the most vulnerable parts of our population, cultivate a sense of victimization, and indulge in conspiracy theories.

Changing that requires more responsible leaders, but we must also work as individuals to break the cycle of accusation, mockery and hatred.

In 1990, the 69-year-old actress, Viveca Lindfors, was mugged in New York City's Greenwich Village. Her attacker razor-slashed her left ear, and it took 29 stitches to repair the damage. The Swedish-born actress had lived in the United States for some time and appeared onstage and in films in numerous roles. I had seen her as Queen Margaret in an avant-garde production of Shakespeare's *Richard III*, in which she cursed her hunchbacked son while smoking a cigarette. Later, she played a memorable, wise old woman in the movie *Stargate*.

The reporters who expected her to lash out or feel victimized were in for a surprise. Lindfors was calm and expressed concern for her assailant. "I'm coming off easily, compared to him," she said. "My ear is cut, but his life is going to be hell if he doesn't face something within himself." Then, she asked, "How do we fight back? How do we struggle against this kind of thing?" and continued, "I only know one way, and that is to keep on performing what is of spiritual value to people. If I could get into schools and read poetry to these kids, couldn't they turn their passion and that turbulence into the strong life force, use this life force in a positive way?"

Perhaps a bit of wishful thinking, but give her credit for trying to address the underlying issues. We all need to find our own ways to respond and affirm what is right and good in us as best we can, especially in times of darkness.

INTERLUDE

SING LOUDER AT THE END

When I first moved to New York, I shared an apartment with Nelson Sheeley and Dennis Kotecki. Nelson, a talented director of comedies, musicals and opera, had attended the Yale School of Drama a decade or so before me. He loved good food, Dvorak's music, and farce.

We agreed that critics hate farce because there is really only one thing to say after attending one of those brash, riotous, anarchic comedies—namely, to answer the yes-no question: Did the production make you laugh so hard you had to hold onto your ribs to keep them from exploding?

Nelson's lover and protégé, Dennis, was a high tenor and a gifted choreographer. I asked him to come to a rehearsal of the first opera I directed to help me with a dance interlude—I have two left feet when it comes to staging such numbers. In 45 minutes, Dennis put together a village dance that was witty, fun and told a story of flirtation and seduction. He gave each chorus members a mini role—mayor, blacksmith, sweetheart, village whore, etc.—and arranged the sequence accordingly.

One of our favorite topics of conversation was about which vocalists we liked and loathed. We distinguished between those singers who can create a character in musical numbers and arias, and those who have great voices and generate a beautiful sound, but not much else. In opera, we favored Maria Callas over Beverly Sills and Joan Sutherland; Placido Domingo over Luciano Pavarotti. In jazz and popular music, we liked Cleo Laine, Billie Holiday and Ella Fitzgerald; Celine Dion, Jennifer Hudson, and Neil Diamond, not so much (although Diamond is a terrific songwriter).

You can always tell the difference between the two approaches by doing a simple experiment. Try to read something—a good novel or challenging article—while listening to someone singing. If you have no trouble comprehending the material, you're hearing a pretty voice that creates soothing background music. But if you can't remember anything you've read, you're in thrall of someone who connects fully to the words of a song instead of just hitting all the notes, however spectacularly. Singers that do the latter capture your attention. You can't take your ears off them.

Our favorite opera star to excoriate was Luciano Pavarotti. This was before he became world famous as one of the Three Tenors, although he was an international household name in the opera world already. You couldn't argue with the man's vocal chords. The sound he produced was gorgeous—his high notes rang out like silver trumpets. But playing even a semi-convincing character onstage was beyond him.

I had seen Pavarotti as Cavaradossi in a production of *Tosca* at the Metropolitan Opera with Montserrat Caballé in the title role. Both hefty singers, they negotiated the stage together like two awkward hippopotamuses and barely managed to touch lips for their culminating kiss in the Act I love duet. I couldn't help snorting with laughter, which drew the ire of a number of devoted audience members. I laughed just as hard at the end of the tragedy when Caballé as Tosca, instead of leaping to her death from the ramparts of Rome's Gandolfo Castle, simply walked offstage. In her triangular shift designed to hide her ample figure, she looked like a bouncing tent. Opera is a silly world despite the sublime music. But that's another story.

When Dennis sang in the Met chorus for two seasons, he had plenty of opportunity to see Pavarotti close up on and offstage, and he detested him. "You could always tell when one of his arias came up," Dennis would say with blistering contempt. "His eyes glazed over and there was nothing going on upstairs when he opened his mouth to sing."

That jibed with my experience of the Italian tenor. I liked him best in his cameo appearance as the Italian Singer in the 1982 Met production of *Der Rosenkavalier*, which suited him perfectly: performing an aria beautifully without any emotion. For Pavarotti's signature aria, "Nessun Dorma," from Puccini's *Turandot*, I much prefer listening to the Swedish tenor Jussi Bjorling.

By the time I met him, Dennis had left the opera world and was pursuing musical comedy under Nelson's tutelage. They were rehearsing various numbers for productions at a summer stock theater in Pennsylvania where Nelson was the artistic director. It was fun and instructive listening to him at the piano coach Dennis. Having been a latecomer to American musical theater—I grew up on operettas in Germany—I was happy to learn from his experience and expertise.

As they practiced, Nelson repeatedly told Dennis, "Sing louder at the end. That will bring the audiences to their feet, and that's what they'll remember. It won't matter if you made mistakes along the way. They'll forgive and forget so long as you sing louder at the end!"

Made a lot of sense to me.

Then, it occurred to me that it's good advice for other situations, too. After all, the squeaky wheel gets the all attention.

And why not go out with a bang instead of a whimper, to reverse T. S. Eliot's phrase from "The Hollow Men" about how the world ends. Rather than take to heart General MacArthur's comment about old soldiers just fading away, why not apply Nelson's advice for musical comedy to your own passing, perhaps with a memorable exit line.

In his poem "Do not go gentle into that good night," Dylan Thomas wrote,

Old age should burn and rage at close of day
Rage, rage against the dying of the light."

I'm with Thomas.

Sing louder at the end!

From the first it has been the theater's business
to entertain people...it needs no other passport than fun.

—Bertolt Brecht, *Little Organum for the Theater*

ACT V–FURTHER MUSINGS

CRITICS ARE PEOPLE, TOO

I was having lunch with an actress who was upset about a bad review. I reminded her of the old theater adage—It doesn't matter whether the review is good or bad, so long as they spell your name right—but she wouldn't have it. "Those who can, do; those who can't, teach; those who can't teach become critics!" she fumed with eloquence born of fury.

Having reviewed plays and movies in my early twenties, I am not so harsh in my judgment. In my experience, most critics are harmless. A few are outstanding. A very few are mean-spirited and dangerous. The first essentially write book reviews that tell the story of the play and comment on sets and costumes. The best provide historical or current insights that enhance an audience's understanding and viewing pleasure. Only a handful are malicious. Drunk on the aphrodisiac of sitting in judgment of others more talented than them, they relish the power to make or break a show.

That doesn't mean I haven't had my run-ins with critics.

When I directed my second opera, *Giuditta*, by Franz Lehar for Bel Canto Opera, I met Richard Traubner, a reviewer for *The New York Times*, at a party held a week before opening. Also in attendance was soprano Jarmila Novotná, then in her 70s, who had sung the title role in the 1934 premiere at the Vienna State Opera.

She shared a photograph from the production, in which her leading tenor, Richard Tauber, had bent her over backward for a passionate, romantic kiss. Her eyes misted up when she spoke of him.

Lehar wrote operettas—the most famous being *The Merry Widow*, but *Giuditta*, his last work, was a more ambitious effort. Scored for a large orchestra, it deals with the ill-fated love affair of a beautiful night-club singer and an Italian army soldier stationed in North Africa. At some point, he deserts to follow her, but she has moved on, leaving him devastated. The music is sultry and sensual like the desert locations. A historical aside: Lehar wanted to dedicate the score to Mussolini, the Italian Fascist dictator, but Il Duce refused the honor, saying, "No soldier in the Italian Army would ever be a deserter."

Richard Traubner, a great fan of operetta had written a substantial book on the subject, *Operetta: A Theatrical History*. I had skimmed the chapter on *Giuditta* in a bookstore. As we got to talking, he asked me if I had read his book. Surrounded by singers and musicians, I joked, "I don't read." His face dropped—not funny. I immediately realized I had put my foot in my mouth, big time, but it was too late.

The review that Traubner wrote in *The New York Times* was surprisingly positive. He praised the production, the singers, even the set, but he didn't mention my name. When I read it, I couldn't help but smile. I knew that the omission—his revenge—was entirely my fault, a self-inflicted wound. All I could do was chalk it up as a learning experience and take the lesson in stride.

Just remember, critics have egos as big as any theater practitioner. That doesn't mean you have to suck up to them; but insulting them, unintentionally or otherwise, is not a good idea.

As promoters, critics serve an essential function, introducing audiences to works they might otherwise ignore. In 1976, I went to see *Comedians* by Trevor Griffith on Broadway. The play concerns a group of young, working-class men in Manchester, England, aspiring to become stand-up comics. Angry and aggressive, it examines politics, sexism and racism—hardly the stuff to please Broadway audiences at the time. But Benedict Nightingale wrote an article in *The New York Times*, extolling a young Jonathan Pryce's "electrifying" performance, and the play ran for 145 performances at the Music Box Theatre.

I spent the afternoon before going to *Comedians* at the Long Island home of my girlfriend's mother. She had seen it already and, in her words, "loved it." She called Pryce's performance "electrifying," not realizing she was quoting the review, but had little else to say about the production. I realized that she would never have bothered attending it if she hadn't read the critic's enthusiastic endorsement.

Few people are willing to take a risk with something unfamiliar. When it comes to new experiences, they prefer them preapproved and certified. It's why sequels, from *Superman II* to *Harry Potter and the Chamber of Secrets*, do better financially after the first movie or book becomes a success. Everyone wants to get on the blockbuster bandwagon. One-time hits like *Titanic* or *Little Miss Sunshine* are rare exceptions. The human herd's preference for accredited, familiar fare is also one of the reasons why critics can wield such extraordinary power and, in many cases, elevate or sink a brand-new work.

Historically, the best critics have championed playwrights, composers and artists who didn't immediately appeal to the middle-class audiences that could afford to see or hear their works. The 19th-century Danish critic, Georg Brandes, formulated the principles of "realism" and paved the way for playwrights like Ibsen and Chekhov. In 1961, Martin Esslin coined the term "Theater of the Absurd," with a book by that title. It legitimized a number of obscure European playwrights for American readers and theater professionals—Samuel Beckett, Jean Genet, Eugene Ionesco, Fernando Arrabal and others.

But ordinary critics rarely have such a wide-ranging perspective. More often than not, they let their personal tastes dominate their acid-tongued reviews. How else to account for a Russian review-er writing in 1875, "Tchaikovsky's First Piano Concerto, like the first pancake, is a flop." Or the notice in the *New York Telegram* on December 14, 1928, calling George Gershwin's *An American in Paris* "nauseous claptrap…dull, patchy, thin, vulgar, long-winded and inane…. This cheap and silly affair seemed pitifully futile and inept."

I remember reading two reviews of *Mrs. Warren's Profession* starring Uta Hagen in the title role at the Roundabout Theater. George Bernard Shaw's play is a powerful social drama about a former prostitute turned brothel owner and respected businesswoman who has to face the reproaches of her liberal daughter. Frank Rich in *The New York Times*, all but kissed the ground under Hagen's feet with his effusive accolades for her performance. In contrast, Clive Barnes in the *New York Post* panned her with a vengeance. I thought that neither critic had attended the play I saw, and they didn't add anything useful to my experience of it. Hagen was marvelous, though. She had prepared the role of Mrs. Warren (her last stage performance) for six months. In the climactic scene when her daughter rejects her, she uttered a rasping, guttural cry, like a wounded animal, and it sent shivers down my spine.

Rich, who was known as "The Butcher of Broadway" for his scathing reviews, at least was able to learn and grow. In 1979, after he panned David Hare's *The Secret Rapture*, the British playwright wrote him an "open" letter that was leaked to the press. Hare did not mince words, accusing Rich of abusing his power. But what I remember most about it was his contention that you could always tell what the *Times* critic was *against* in the theater, but never what he was *for*. Rich defended himself in a letter of his own, but he subsequently included more explanations for his opinions and pronouncements in his reviews. He took on the role of educator, not just malicious, slash-and-burn columnist. Since hanging up his critic spurs, he has become a thoughtful and incisive essayist, commentator on politics and social issues, and television producer of such shows as *Veep* and *Succession*.

Another theater critic at the time, John Simon, writing for *New York Magazine*, was notorious for reviewing not only plays and movies but also the performers' physical attributes. He was particularly vicious toward female actors. He once wrote that Barbra Streisand's nose "cleaves the giant screen from east to west, bisects it from north to south. It zigzags across our horizon like a bolt of fleshy lightning." The man clearly had issues.

Harvard-educated, Simon knew a great deal about literature and theater, and could have been an outstanding commentator, but he chose to fritter away his gifts by obsessively focusing on actors' looks.

When I was with the ANTA company in Chautauqua in upstate New York, Michael Kahn, the artistic director of the Acting Company, also in residence there, invited Simon to come and talk to the young actors in both companies. I have no memory of what Simon said, but I do recall him sitting hunched over in a chair in the middle of the room, at a safe distance from the attendees, with his hands in his lap as if to protect his groin against attacks. I almost felt sorry for him.

That critiquing the physical appearance of actors was such a controversial issue seems a bit quaint nowadays, considering the length to which performers go to improve their looks. Hollywood stars get face lifts, butt lifts, breast enlargements, Botox and other kinds of cosmetic augmentation to keep their bodies, lips and hair in top shape. Some use doubles for nude scenes to hide their embarrassment or to project a more perfect image than they could manage on their own.

The practice of physical enhancement in the service of beautification is as old as civilization. During the Restoration period in England, men's calves were considered sexy. The rakes, wearing shoes with heels, would strike a pose, either sitting or standing, and prominently display a muscular leg, usually on the side opposite to where their sword dangled, to attract the attention and compliments of female onlookers. A cottage industry sprung up for making leather prosthetics that could be slipped beneath the stockings by men who were not naturally endowed with beefy calves.

When I directed *The Provok'd Wife*, this became useful knowledge I passed on to the male cast members, who started to practice preening with their legs. To get them acclimated to walking in heels, I asked the costume designer to provide period footwear from the start of rehearsals so they could practice their stances. For the first week, they all complained about being "in shoe hell."

While conventional physical beauty matters, it is not the defining characteristic of success in the theater and film world. Otherwise wonderful actors like Maggie Gyllenhaal, Toni Collette, Hillary Swank and Tilda Swinton would not get starring roles.

As for critics, in the age on the Internet, none wield power the way Walter Kerr, Frank Rich, Roger Ebert or Pauline Kael did in their heydays. Most fans checking out *Rotten Tomatoes* look at the percentage rating. Even if they scan some of the excerpts of various bloggers and traditional critics, they rarely click to read the full review. At the same time, word of mouth has become the biggest purveyor of all for critical judgments. Negative postings on Twitter, Facebook and Instagram can sink a movie that opens on a Thursday by the weekend.

In time, critics as we know them may become obsolete. Until then, treat them politely and with kindness. They generally don't have a sense of humor and take themselves way too seriously. Their feelings can get hurt, although they rarely admit it. But the best will be thoughtful, informative, revelatory and eloquent, and it behooves you to have them on your side.

POLITICS

In May of 1993, Edward Albee came to Florida Studio Theatre to speak at the Young Playwrights' Festival. Every fall, actors from FST would travel to schools throughout Florida with a 45-minute show that demonstrated the elements of drama. They encouraged students to pen five-minute plays and send them to the theater. Led by Kate Alexander, then head of FST's education department, the Write-A-Play program kept growing until we received more than 5,000 submissions a year.

To cull the abundance of plays, we conducted staff read-a-thons. As Associate Director for New Plays, I made the final selections and gave them to Kate and Artistic Director Richard Hopkins for approval. The winning entries received story theater-style productions called *Under 6* and *7 Up*. I directed the latter—the middle and high school plays—during the program's inaugural season.

For the Young Playwrights' Festival in May, we invited the young authors and their families to come to a special performance of their works and attend an awards ceremony. Some had never set foot inside a theater or seen a live performance before. They and their parents arrived wearing their Sunday best, looking intimidated and frightened, uncertain what they were in for. Once the show started, they all relaxed and enjoyed themselves.

To give Write-A-Play a boost in the community and beyond, we wanted a well-known, keynote speaker for the awards ceremony. We were fortunate to book Edward Albee, at the time considered America's greatest living playwright, although he couldn't get a production in New York—this was the year before he won his third Pulitzer Prize for *Three Tall Women*. He was available and affordable and enjoyed his time with us so much that he returned the following two years and gave FST permission to be one of the first regional theaters to produce *Three Tall Women* after its New York run.

When Albee came to Sarasota that first May, he was amazed by the quality of the works. In their short pieces, the young playwrights had reinvented all theatrical forms, going back to the ancient Greeks—comedy, tragedy, farce, romance. When Albee told them at the awards ceremony that he had enjoyed their plays more than most of what he saw on Broadway, the youngsters were surprised and captivated. For many, it was the first time that they received recognition and accolades for something they had done, and by a famous person no less!

That evening, Albee addressed an adult audience in a fundraiser for the theater. Sarasota has a large number of wealthy retirees who support the arts and other worthy causes with unbridled generosity. Non-profits raise more than $600 million each year, an astonishing figure considering that Sarasota is a relatively small community, and it speaks volumes about financially successful people willing to give back.

It so happens that many of them are Republicans.

As "theater angels," they were pleased to meet such a renowned playwright and eager to hear what he had to say. Some came decked out in evening gowns and tuxedos. They warmed to Albee when he discussed the state of the arts in America and mentioned his patronage for young sculptors and painters—he made part of his house in Montauk, Long Island, available as a retreat for them and purchased some of their works.

Then, he said, "I have traveled all over this country and met artists everywhere, and I hate to tell you this, but most creative people are Democrats."

Needless to say, that comment dropped on the attendees like a stink bomb and they guffawed and grumbled. A few outraged patrons got up and walked out. Their ire was understandable. They felt that Albee had insulted them. And he had. He knew exactly what he was doing!

The question, however, remains: Was Albee right? Are artists, as a group, more liberal than the rest of society?

We know that conservative politicians like to rail against the leftist Hollywood elite. The American culture wars are far from over. They go into hibernation for a season or two, but conservatives still campaign to eliminate the National Endowment of the Arts, even though it has a piddling annual budget of $160 million, barely enough to launch one cruise missile! More recently, Donald Trump reignited the culture wars with his attacks on Colin Kaepernick for kneeling during the national anthem to protest police brutality against African Americans.

When I was at the Yale School of Drama during the Reagan years, there were two students in the acting program who openly professed to be Republicans. I won't name names, but one had a trust fund and was voted by his class "Actor Least Needing to Succeed," and the other was a first-generation American actress from the Midwest (children of immigrants are often more gung-ho conservative than their parents). If there were others, they chose to fly under the radar. In general, when politics came up at all, most expressed liberal sentiments. But such discussions were infrequent. Actors and theater graduate students are more self-centered and worried about their careers.

There were also aspects of the training that affirmed a more liberal, all-embracing approach to life. In the first-year acting class,

I remember Earle Gister discussing how to bridge the gap between the present and the past in order to get inside the characters created by Ibsen and Chekhov. He said, "People are people wherever you go." By this he meant that they have the same desires, fears, loves, needs—a humanistic assertion that encouraged us to see beyond our differences.

Having studied anthropology and possessing personal insight into some fundamental differences between German and American culture, I held my tongue. But in many ways, he was right. Even 100 years later, we all could find something to relate to in these Norwegian and Russian characters and identify with the frustrations, hopes and dreams of Nora Helmer, Hedda Gabler, master builder Halvard Solness, the three sisters Masha, Olga and Irina, Uncle Vanya, Nina, Madame Arkadina, and Madame Ranevskaya.

I can only hope that some of the training and subsequent experiences in the theater rubbed off on my more conservative peers. When you come right down to it, much of cultural politics and ideology is personal. After all, even former Vice President Dick Cheney, the Darth Vader of the Bush administration, kept mum when his reactionary peers bashed gay rights because he has a lesbian daughter.

Conservatives tend to divide the world into us and them, haves and have-nots, and like it that way. Many actors and other artists identify with groups of people who, for whatever reason—racism, poverty, famine, wartime dislocation—are outsiders, disenfranchised and downtrodden.

Why would that be the case? I have long suspected that it has to do with the fact that many creative people carry childhood wounds as a result of divorce or a parent dying, as just about every interview by James Lipton on *Inside the Actor's Studio* revealed. As a result, artists often feel alienated in many aspects of their lives. As outsiders and fringe members of society, they identify with others in analogous situations.

That is not to say there aren't some conservatives with talent and compassion. But, for every Jon Voight or Clint Eastwood on the Right, there are ten liberal Jane Fondas, Sean Penns and Steven Spielbergs. And let's face it, unlike Sarasota and a few other pockets in the United States, where an unusual number of moderate Republicans support "worthy causes," you don't hear of a lot of successful, conservative actors going to Haiti, New Orleans, or Puerto Rico to offer help after hurricanes and other natural disasters.

This goes to the heart of what is required to create good, lasting art. Yes, there have been fascist artists with tremendous gifts, like the Nazi filmmaker Leni Riefenstahl. But there were many more brilliant artists labeled "degenerate," who fled Hitler's Germany or perished in the concentration camps, than state-approved writers, painters and composers. Similarly, in Stalin's Russia, socialist realism was legislated by committee, but little of what it produced ranks as more than a footnote in cultural history. None of the party hacks in fascist or communist societies who obeyed their governments' rules were of the caliber of Thomas Mann, Bertolt Brecht, Herman Hesse, Sergei Prokofiev, Dmitri Shostakovich, and all the creative people who ended up in Hollywood: directors Billy Wilder and Fred Zinnemann; composers Erich Wolfgang Korngold and Kurt Weill; and actors Marlene Dietrich, Lotte Lenya, Peter Lorre and Paul Henreid, to name a few.

Albee was right when he tweaked the egos of the well-intentioned conservatives of Sarasota's social elite.

FAME

In 1984 when I moved to New York, Bill Kux sublet me his room in an apartment in Chelsea. He had gotten a job in a production of *Crimes of the Heart* by Beth Henley in a limited engagement at the Birmingham Theater, a large performance venue outside of Detroit. The Pulitzer Prize-winning play is a southern gothic comedy about a trio of sisters with a penchant for trouble who reunite at their Mississippi home after the youngest, Babe, shoots her abusive husband.

Bill, who is equally adept at comedy, drama and musicals, played Barnett Lloyd, the lawyer who has a big crush on Babe. The producers held rehearsals in New York City, then took the play to Detroit.

The star of the show was Genie Francis, who had been a regular on *General Hospital* as a teenager. She'd played Laura Spencer, one of the most beloved daytime television characters of all times—her on-screen wedding to Luke Spencer commanded an audience of 30 million people! When she turned 21, she decided that she wanted to be a legitimate actress. She left Hollywood for New York, took acting lesson and landed the role of Babe.

Every performance during the run sold out. Many of the young girls in the audience shouted "We love you, Laura!" as soon as she made her entrance. Afterward, some ventured backstage to catch a glimpse of their idol. Bill never heard them compliment Genie on her performance, which he said was delightful, or even mention that they had seen the play. It was always, "When are you coming back to *General Hospital?*" or repetitions of their interjections during the play, "We love you, Laura!"

The cast members became quite friendly and spent much of their free time together because they enjoyed each other's company and Genie's fans were so persistent and intrusive. One afternoon, they all went to Toys R Us to find some board games to play during their time off. Word spread through the store that "Laura" was shopping, and when they got to the checkout counter, they were met by a crowd of Genie's fans, all wide-eyed and excited. Everyone wanted an autograph (this was before selfies), but no one had any paper. So, the intrepid idol worshipers began to tear up shopping bags and receipts and thrust them at Genie.

Subsequently, some of the cast members joked that if they ever wanted to cause a small riot in suburban Detroit's Tel-Twelve Mall, all they had to do was let Genie loose and shout, "Laura's here!"

Genie may have been a soap opera superstar, but she was also a hard-working actress. Besides nightly performances and matinees, she spent several hours a day managing her career. She gave radio and television interviews, replied to fan mail, and was ever gracious with people that approached her.

When the tour ended and Bill returned to New York, he told me, "I've seriously reconsidered my idea of the kind of career I want for myself."

He'd gotten a first-hand look at stardom and didn't like the disconcerting aspects of fame. He has worked steadily as an actor ever since, appearing in a number of films and television shows, but his primary focus has been doing plays on- and off-Broadway and in regional theaters.

Few have the opportunity to experience the demands of fame and stardom beforehand. For most, when it comes, it descends overnight, and its recipients are rarely prepared for the downside. Before long, they have an entourage that includes minders, publicists, agents and bodyguards. Perhaps the greatest price of fame is loss of privacy as fans seeking their attention feel they own a piece of them.

Ever since John Hinkley became pathologically obsessed with Jodi Foster and attempted to assassinate President Reagan to impress her, many actors are understandably paranoid when accosted in public. Some can be quite standoffish.

Of course, most fans aren't stalkers, but few know the best way to act in the presence of one of their idols. I learned the proper way to approach famous people from Maximilian Schell, an Austrian-born actor, director and writer, who had a significant international career. He did an acclaimed version of *Hamlet* for German television, won an Academy Award for his portrayal of a ruthless defense attorney in the film *Judgement at Nuremberg*, and directed *Marlene*, a remarkable documentary film about Marlene Dietrich that deals, among other things, with the ephemeral nature of fame and beauty.

Schell was a good friend of Joseph Albers, the painter and educator, whose famous series *Homage to the Square* demonstrated his theory that colors deceive and change depending on their surroundings. He was a member of the arts faculty at Yale, and when he died in 1976, Schell attended a commemorative gathering held in a small lecture room at the Yale University Art Gallery. He read from Albers' journals, talked about their friendship, and revealed Albers as a much more interesting man than his paintings of squares within squares suggested (although some of them have sold for more than $1 million since).

In front of me sat two young female art students who were quite taken with Schell, who was a very handsome man. Hemming and hawing, they finally gathered their courage to go up to him afterward. I followed behind and overheard their conversation with Schell, who spoke English fluently.

When they told him how nervous they were and didn't know whether or not to approach a famous person like him, he smiled. With a humorous twinkle, he said, "You always should feel free to walk up to people in the public eye. Here is how you do it: You say, 'My name is so and so. I am so glad to meet you. I wanted to thank you for your work. It has given me a great deal of pleasure.' Then you shake hands and move on."

I must admit I was a bit star-struck, too. So, when it was my turn, I took his advice and told him how much I had enjoyed him in *Topkapi*, a wonderful heist movie set in Istanbul. When I mentioned that I had grown up in Germany, he switched to German and introduced me to his sister, Maria Schell, who was sitting in the front row. She was an international film star, too—her best-known American movies were *Cimarron* with Glenn Ford, *The Odessa File*, and the first *Superman* movie. All I remember was that she was lovely and gracious, and that she had a long age line that crossed her face diagonally but didn't mar her beauty one bit.

Unable to tear myself away, I accompanied Schell on the way out of the room. At some point, he turned to me and said, "Nice meeting you." Then he shook my hand and walked on. The encounter was over.

This occurred before I went to drama school to become a director, but it taught me how to approach famous people as human beings. The key is to act neither threatening nor obsequious but to let them know how much you appreciate them and their work. Nine times out of ten, they will be cordial.

Here is an example of how not to do it. My friend Michael Schiemann had an encounter with Jason Robarts on the streets of New York. Robarts had played Hickey in Eugene O'Neill's *The Iceman Cometh* in a famous off-Broadway production and originated the role of James Tyrone in *Long Day's Journey* into Night on Broadway.

He is best known for his Academy Award-winning portrayal of Ben Bradlee, the crusty editor of the *Washington Post* during the Watergate investigation, in the film *All the President's Men*.

Michael was so tickled, he yelled out, "Hey, Jase!" walked up to him, and engaged him in conversation. Robarts was polite, betraying none of the impatience he probably felt. At some point, it occurred to Michael that he'd been rather presumptuous, and he asked, "Do you mind it when people just come up to you on the street?"

Robarts chuckled and said, "No, it comes with the territory." Then he switched to his low-octave, baritone voice and growled, "But don't ever call me Jase again!" and stalked off.

For all the hoopla and accolades, fame is fleeting. In the words of Emily Dickinson, "Fame is a fickle food upon a shifting plate." Even these days when everything people create finds its way onto the Internet—books, paintings, songs, movies, personal musings, selfies, and videos of their cats and dogs—the memories of fans and admirers are short.

Ask anyone under 30 about Clark Gable, Carole Lombard, Claudette Colbert, William Powell or Mae West—all at various times the highest paid actors in Hollywood. Unless they are in the film industry themselves or old movie buffs who like to watch TCM, they'll probably look at you in puzzlement and shrug.

I've tested this out on my 29-year-old son Erik. The only actors from the silent film era and early talkies he knows are Buster Keaton and the Marx Brothers because he and I watched their movies together when he was young. He loved Keaton's inimitable slapstick and Groucho's wit and physical antics. Erik won't look at other black and white films as a matter of principle. To him, they're old-fashioned and passé.

There are a few creative artists who have lasted. Shakespeare wrote that his sonnets would make him immortal. But it is his plays that have kept his name in public awareness for more than 400 years. Just about everybody knows "To be or not to be," probably the most famous line ever written, on par with "Ta-da-da-dah," the opening to Beethoven's *Fifth Symphony*.

But that level of fame is rare, like making it to "The Show" in baseball—being called up from the minors to the major leagues. Or becoming a household name for a while, like Picasso, The Beatles, Michael Jordan, and Muhammad Ali. Certain U.S. presidents belong in that category, as do some notorious figures of evil like Jack the Ripper and Adolf Hitler. The current crop of political talking heads and sports and entertainment gods are lionized, of course. But you have to wonder how long anyone will remember Sean Hannity, Rachel Maddow, LeBron James, Tom Brady, Beyoncé, Jay-Z or Kim Kardashian.

So, if fame won't buy you immortality, what are the alternatives? The pursuit of money and power are two aphrodisiacs that have become enshrined in some economic systems, notably western capitalism. Buying lots of things is another. But none of them offers a firm foundation to stand on in the long run or gives lasting meaning to our lives.

The United States consumes more than a third of the painkiller drugs in the world. Yet, binging on pharmaceuticals has not made its citizens any happier. More people than ever suffer from depression. The angry, divisive politics of fear and condemnation practiced by so many of our putative leaders represents the other side of that coin. A discussion of why this is so would take another book. Suffice it to say, in the words of the poet Frank O'Hara, "Pain always produces logic, which is very bad for you."

One of my college roommates wrote a philosophy paper on "the meaningless of death to the dead." His professor flunked him. But the point is well-taken. What matters is what we do with our lives.

What comes after—who cares? That's why I don't scoff at people who spend a good portion of their days on Facebook and Instagram, and follow others, more famous than them, on Twitter. Yes, there are times when I want to say, "Get a life," but who am I to judge?

The need to feel important, to believe that one's life has meaning, that there is a greater purpose than ourselves, is very powerful. Science since Darwin and Einstein has taken that certainty away from us. If religion doesn't provide the assurance you crave, why not take selfies and itemize your day-to-day experiences, however mundane, and post them on various social networks? Feeling significant—that we matter—seems to be a fundamental human desire, along with the pain and pleasure principles articulated by Sigmund Freud.

The ability to divert us from such heady and angst-inducing thoughts, I believe, is one of the reasons people get hooked on acting and directing in the theater and the movies. Besides the accolades and money in film and television, and the high of a theatrical performance, being able to enter into another character is wonderfully distracting from one's inadequacies and existential anguish.

For directors, the push to get a play to performance can take up every bit of time and energy. In film, it's not unusual to spend 18- to 20-hour days on a movie set. Making decisions, planning for the next day's shoot, coping with different personalities, and troubleshooting when things don't go as expected is exhilarating and all-consuming. Many directors collapse in exhaustion after the wrap party and can't get out of bed for a week. Once they recover and have edited the film, they can't wait to go on to the next project.

In the theater, tech week and previews are similarly frenetic and engrossing. Whatever problems you may have with your lover, your wife or children, or the IRS, can be—must be—set aside until opening. That is your mission and get-out-of-jail-free card to deny the demands of ordinary existence and the fear of oblivion once you're gone.

As an evanescent endeavor, the theater is more dangerously and cruelly human than the movies. Yes, you can make videos of productions to capture them for posterity, but more often than not, plays and performances linger on only in the memories of the participants and audiences. They're ephemeral.

As Leonard Nimoy, the original Dr. Spock on *Star Trek*, tweeted shortly before he died, "A life is like a garden. Perfect moments can be had, but not preserved, except in memory."

Still, the creative process, whether you're writing, painting, composing, acting, gardening, scrapbooking—you name it—provides pleasure and can give meaning to one's existence.

As the American painter Larry Rivers said late in life, "When I was younger I always wanted to *be* somebody, now I just want to *do*."

SO YOU WANT TO BE AN ACTOR

Recently, I saw an exhibit of works by Nathan Sawayer, an internationally acclaimed Lego artist—some of his sculptures contain more than 80,000 pieces. In the introductory video, he talked about how he majored in art in college and then, like many budding artists, went to law school. After becoming increasingly unhappy as a corporate attorney, he lucked out when his evening hobby—playing creatively with Legos—took off and he was able to quit his day job.

In my time as a director, I met many attorneys who didn't enjoy practicing law. A surprising number were either closet writers or actor wannabes. Some of them were quite good. But they didn't pursue their talent because paying their dues would have required them to start out at a subbasement income instead of the six-figure salaries they were earning. A few became litigators and acted out their thespian fantasies in the courtroom before judges and juries.

One of the better workshop productions we presented at Florida Studio Theatre was *Getting and Spending* by Michael J. Chepiga, then a senior partner at a prestigious New York law firm. It took him several years to write the play because he had little free time. For two weeks over the Christmas holidays, he and his family went to the Colorado Rocky Mountains. Michael hated skiing, and while his wife and kids hit the slopes, he stayed behind in the hotel room and wrote. The play was promising and eventually received a Broadway production. Michael wrote a few other plays, but he never felt he could afford to give up his lucrative day job.

Another story: On a stop at Kansas State University in Manhattan, Kansas—the "Little Apple"—the ANTA Touring Company performed *A History of American Film*, a musical by Christopher Durang. Afterward, the cast and I attended a party in our honor at the house of a wealthy local banker. At some point, the host cornered me and told me how much he'd enjoyed the show. He may have had one too many because he added, morosely, "I wish I could do what you do, travel all over the country doing something you love."

Here was a successful, wealthy man in his 50s who had serious regrets. I don't know why; I didn't ask. But I was old enough to imagine why he was unhappy. I was 30 when I arrived at the Yale School of Drama and knew what it felt like to be stuck in a job I didn't cherish, although teaching in an alternative public school with a group of smart, caring, dedicated people was an experience I would not want to have missed. When I decided to follow my dreams, I didn't have a family yet, so switching career horses in midstream didn't cause upheaval in any life other than my own.

And I can say without hesitation that it was one of the best decisions I ever made.

So, when younger people ask me for career advice, I always counsel them to do something they love and enjoy. Better to throw your hat in the ring and get smacked around a bit than to have regrets later on. The experiences you gather in the school of hard knocks will come in handy in whatever career you decide to pursue. And always remember: persistence is the most important ingredient in achieving success.

On the other hand, it's never too late to heed the siren call of artistic endeavor. Rosalie Sorrels, a mother of five, left her marriage and home in Utah to become a folk and country singer in New York City. She took her kids with her and made a go of it. There are many stories about people who have a successful second or third career in retirement—no rest for the talented. If you're a guy, remember, the theater and movies always need good, older character men!

We're told that with globalization and the changes in the workplace ushered in by computers, robots and artificial intelligence, few of us can count on having just one occupation during our lifetime. More than likely, we'll have seven or more different jobs. The practices that theater and film encourage—acquiring new skills, nurturing flexibility, and cultivating a sense of curiosity, will surely prove useful in that brave new world.

So, why not have some fun, especially when you're young and unencumbered, and take the artistic path, if that is what you want to do? If the theater, film or Lego gods smile on you, they will take you to incredible, wondrous places. And, with luck, John Houseman's words will come true: Everything you want will happen.

Shakespeare knew this over 400 years ago when he had Cassius say to Brutus in *Julius Caesar*:

There is a tide in the affairs of men
Which, taken at the flood, leads on to fortune;
Omitted, all the voyage of their life
Is bound in shallows and in miseries.

So, embrace whatever fear you have about pursuing a financially less than lucrative life for a while. If need be, keep your day job as you follow your dreams and move forward with joy, confidence and abandon.

Sometimes you need a push—I did. But you can also figure out how to fly on your own, or at least know what you want and pursue it with everything you've got. Before you realize it, you'll float like a butterfly, sting like a bee and soar like an eagle.

And always remember: Sing louder at the end!

EPILOGUE

When people ask me why I left the theater, I usually tell them one of two stories.

Around the time my son Erik was four years old, I worked with a 40-year-old actor who threw a childish temper tantrum in rehearsal. I dealt with it—there was no malice on his part—but afterward, I realized I was getting tired of being the daddy of productions. What was appropriate behavior for a frustrated child didn't wear so well with an adult.

The other story concerns my son as well. When he was young and I worked at Florida Studio Theatre, May was the busiest time of year. With the Young Playwrights Festival, a New Play Festival, and the start of the summer mainstage season, we once opened seven shows in five weeks. I was in charge of overseeing both production and play development and didn't have a day off for a month. When I finally came up for air, I noticed that Erik had grown in my absence. The realization came as a shock. When you live with someone day-to-day, you don't register changes like that.

By then, I no longer enjoyed being employed at a regional theater. As a freelancer, you focus on one production. You're usually in residence away from home and can concentrate on what you're doing without interference, giving it your all. As a staff member at a theater as busy as FST, I had to wear several hats, dividing my attention and energy. Also, the place had a strong singles culture. Of the few married staff members, I was the only one with a kid. No one there understood what it was like trying to juggle being a good parent and fulfilling the demands of the job.

Nearly a decade earlier I'd had an epiphany close to the opening of a production of Tina Howe's *Painting Churches*. It's a sweet play of reconciliation about a daughter coming to terms with her aging parents as she helps them pack up their house so they can move to a smaller place. Watching the dress rehearsal, I understood that I had accomplished all I ever wanted to do as a director—figuratively reunite my parents who had gotten divorced when I was four. At that age, you feel responsible for the break-up, no matter what people tell you. To make my family whole again, if only onstage in the fantasy world of a play, felt very gratifying.

Although I continued in the theater for some time and directed several excellent productions, I found the work no longer as involving. My heart just wasn't in it. The opportunity to express something I felt deeply didn't come along often. I was a hired hand and rarely had he opportunity to pick the play I directed. While I always did my job professionally, my career was no longer fulfilling.

I never had the desire to become an artistic director, which would have allowed me to call all the shots—supposedly. The reality is more complicated. While you get to choose the season of plays and can pick which ones you want to direct, you have many other obligations—being the boss of a large staff, dealing with disgruntled patrons, schmoozing donors and staying involved with the community. I understood myself well enough to know that these job requirements would have proven too much of a distraction.

In any case, since I was no longer passionate about directing, it was time to leave the theater. The transition wasn't easy. It's difficult to let go of something that has occupied most of your waking (and sleeping) existence and find something else that engages you fully. I went through a lengthy period of mourning, working at jobs that didn't satisfy me to support my family. When I reemerged, I decided to pursue writing, which I had wanted to do since high school. My early efforts at fiction weren't memorable. I didn't have anything to say. Now, I had a wealth of experience to draw on.

Once again, when I could articulate what I really wanted, doors opened I didn't know existed. Over the past decade, I have had my hands in more than 70 books, including ghostwriting seven novels and memoirs, as well as writing hundreds of articles for different magazines and newspapers. I have no regrets about making the change. I find writing, editing and bookmaking as absorbing and creatively challenging as directing, and it has a lot fewer hassles.

At the same time, I continue to appreciate many things my theatrical sojourn taught me.

Although I am generally soft-spoken, I can easily dial up my vocal volume to 11 (in a nod to *Spinal Tap* and Christopher Guest's marvelous turn as fictitious rock legend Nigel Tufnel). With full diaphragm support, I don't get hoarse shouting at the top of my voice.

I have an undying curiosity about what makes others tick—be they of different gender, ethnic background or culture—and I appreciate the differences rather than let them frighten me.

I have an eye for the dramatic and always encourage writers to go for broke, remembering that it is easier to pull back an over-the-top performance than to invigorate an anemic presentation late in the game. As an editor and coach, I can tell when writers back away from uncomfortable material they don't wish to reveal but which is right for their characters. And I can often help them allay their fears so they can let themselves go there.

After all, dramatists, novelists and other writers share a number of qualities. They're often fun, witty people with a wide range of interests and a lot of weird, arcane knowledge about the oddest things. They make enjoyable dinner conversationalists and drinking companions. In general, directors like Scotch while writers prefer Bourbon, although these days there are a lot more wine and beer drinkers in both camps. When it gets close to publication date, writers of books are just like playwrights on opening night—thrilled, excited, scared to death, and often quite hammered.

Ultimately, though, it is their attention to telling details, insistence on finding the exact word for the appropriate moment, and rigorous care about getting the story right that sets them apart from amateur scribblers. Only poets are more obsessive about language. I share that obsession proudly.

On occasion, I still give feedback to playwrights who want me to read their script in progress—I think of playwriting as acting on the page—but for the most part, I have moved on. I don't go to the theater much anymore. For me to be engaged, a performance has to clock in at 100%, not 80%, and that rarely happens. I prefer watching a crappy movie to a so-so play production any time. Besides, these days some of the best dramatic writing is on television, in part because many playwrights have gone to Hollywood, following the lure of better money and potentially larger audiences.

Still, the entertainment industry all need stories and characters from which to develop the scripts that film directors and actors can realize. Novels, articles, and short stories often provide the foundational narratives for movies and TV shows—from *Roots, The Expanse, True Blood, Outlander, Big Little Lies, The Hunger Games* to *Crazy Rich Asians.* (Remember how much better *Game of Thrones* was in the seasons directly based on Geerge R. R. Martin's books than when television writers took over the narrative toward the end.)

In any case, that's where I come in, both in my own efforts and in my work with other writers, keeping the creative spark alive.

In my youth, I was infatuated with the ending of James Joyce's *A Portrait of the Artist as a Young Man,* in which Stephen Daedalus says, "I go to encounter for the millionth time the reality of experience and to forge in the smithy of my soul the uncreated conscience of my race…"

As I am getting older, the lines from Tennyson's "Ulysses" speak to me:

Tho' much is taken, much abides; and tho'
We are not now that strength which in old days
Moved earth and heaven, that which we are, we are;
One equal temper of heroic hearts,
Made weak by time and fate, but strong in will
To strive, to seek, to find, and not to yield.

But what really inspires me is the story of Enrico Dandolo, the 11th-century doge of Venice who fought political and economic battles against the Byzantine Empire for much of his life. In 1202, at age 95, he participated in the Fourth Crusade that ultimately sacked Constantinople. By then, he was stone-blind, but he roused his troops during the assault and, along with their Frankish allies, breached the monumental city walls.

That night, as Constantinople was burning, Dandalo could be seen high on the ramparts illuminated by the flickering flames, swinging his sword over his head and dancing.

Can't sing much louder than that!

&

ACKNOWLEDGMENTS

Theater and film are collaborative arts. Although there have been efforts to replace actors with digitalized versions—Golem in the *Lord of the Ring* films and all those apes who will take over our planet—the long lists of animators, stunt men and women, and techies after the end of a movie speaks volumes about much labor is involved.

There are too many people to thank who contributed to this book, directly and indirectly, but I want to mention a few:

A special thank you goes to Steve Hendrickson, Martin LaPlatney, Bill Kux and Howard Millman for looking over my versions of the stories they told me, correcting and refreshing my memory.

Rick Davis was kind enough to provide astute, "dramaturgical" suggestions, laced with his inimitable sense of humor.

Ed Linehan, Daniel Rubin and Bill Russini read an early incarnation of the manuscript and offered valuable advice.

My wife Susan, who is my most astute and critical reader, contributed many helpful comments and insights along the way.

If I misremembered other tales in this book, it is entirely my fault, and I hope that those concerned forgive me in the spirit of never letting the truth get in the way of a good story.

Any factual errors are my own as well.

INDEX

Journalist, editor, publisher, professional director of theater, opera and musicals, English teacher, carpenter, and cabbie for the Terminal Taxi Company in New Haven, Connecticut (a six-month's gig in a former time warp), **Chris Angermann** has enjoyed a multitude of careers. He has been editor-in-chief for New Chapter Publisher, a small, independent press in Sarasota, Florida, and helps authors self-publish under the imprint Bardolf & Company. Over the past decade, he has had his hands in producing more than 70 books, a number of which have won national awards. He served as president of the Florida Authors Publishers Association (FAPA) for five years, and is the author of an award-winning, anti-self-help book: *How to Mess with Others for Their Own Good.*

For more information go to:

www.chrisangermann.com
www.bardolfandcompany.com